THE
GREAT
DISAPPEARANCE

HOW TO BE RAPTURE READY

STUDY GUIDE | SIXTEEN LESSONS

DR. DAVID JEREMIAH

HarperChristian
Resources

The Great Disappearance Bible Study Guide
© 2023 David P. Jeremiah
P.O. Box 3838, San Diego, CA 92163

Published in Grand Rapids, Michigan, by HarperChristian Resources. HarperChristian Resources
is a registered trademark of HarperCollins Christian Publishing, Inc.

Requests for information should be sent to customercare@harpercollins.com.

ISBN 978-0-310-16794-5 (softcover)
ISBN 978-0-310-16795-2 (ebook)

All Scripture quotations, unless otherwise indicated, are taken from the New King James Version®.
© 1982 by Thomas Nelson. Used by permission. All rights reserved.

Scripture quotations marked CSB® are taken from the Christian Standard Bible®, Copyright © 2017
by Holman Bible Publishers. Used by permission. Christian Standard Bible®, and CSB®, are federally
registered trademarks of Holman Bible Publishers.

Scripture quotations marked KJV are taken from the King James Version. Public domain.

Scripture quotations marked NIV are taken from the Holy Bible, New International Version®,
NIV®. Copyright © 1973, 1978, 1984, 2011 by Biblica, Inc.® Used by permission of Zondervan.
All rights reserved worldwide. www.Zondervan.com. The "NIV" and "New International Version"
are trademarks registered in the United States Patent and Trademark Office by Biblica, Inc.®

Scripture quotations marked NLT are taken from the Holy Bible, New Living Translation. © 1996,
2004, 2015 by Tyndale House Foundation. Used by permission of Tyndale House Publishers, Inc.,
Carol Stream, Illinois 60188. All rights reserved.

Any internet addresses (websites, blogs, etc.) and telephone numbers in this study guide are offered
as a resource. They are not intended in any way to be or imply an endorsement by HarperChristian
Resources, nor does HarperChristian Resources vouch for the content of these sites and numbers
for the life of this study guide.

All rights reserved. No portion of this book may be reproduced, stored in a retrieval system,
or transmitted in any form or by any means—electronic, mechanical, photocopy, recording,
scanning, or other—except for brief quotations in critical reviews or articles, without the prior
written permission of the publisher.

HarperChristian Resources titles may be purchased in bulk for church, business, fundraising,
or ministry use. For information, please e-mail ResourceSpecialist@ChurchSource.com.

Published in association with Yates & Yates, www.yates2.com.

First Printing October 2023 / Printed in the United States of America

CONTENTS

HOW TO USE THIS STUDY GUIDE

The purpose of this study guide is to reinforce Dr. David Jeremiah's dynamic, in-depth teaching and to aid you in applying biblical truth to your daily life. This study guide is designed to be used in conjunction with *The Great Disappearance* by Dr. David Jeremiah, but it may also be used by itself for personal or group study.

Structure of the Lessons

Each lesson is based on the corresponding chapter in *The Great Disappearance* and focuses on specific passages in the Bible. Each lesson is composed of the following elements:

- **Outline**: The outline at the beginning of the lesson gives a clear, concise picture of the topic being studied and provides a helpful framework for readers as they listen to Dr. Jeremiah's teaching.

- **Overview**: The overview summarizes Dr. Jeremiah's teaching on the passage being studied in the lesson. You should refer to the Scripture passages in your own Bible as you study the overview. Unless otherwise indicated, Scripture verses quoted are taken from the *New King James Version*.

- **Application:** This section contains a variety of individual and group discussion questions that are designed to help you dig deeper into the lesson and the Scriptures and to apply the lesson to your daily life. For Bible study groups or Sunday school classes, these questions will provide a springboard for group discussion and interaction.

- **Did You Know?** This section presents a fascinating fact, historical note, or insight that adds a point of interest to the preceding lesson.

Personal Study

The lessons in the *Great Disappearance Study Guide* were created to help you gain fresh insights into God's Word and develop new perspectives on topics you may have previously studied. Each lesson is designed to challenge your thinking and help you grow in your knowledge of Christ. During your study, it is our prayer that you will discover how biblical truth affects every aspect of your life and your relationship with Christ will be strengthened.

When you commit to completing this study guide, try to set apart a time, daily or weekly, to read through the lessons without distraction. Have your Bible nearby when you read the study guide so you're ready to look up verses if you need to. If you want to use a notebook to write down your thoughts, be sure to have that handy as well. Take your time to think through and answer the questions. If you plan on reading the study guide with a small group, be sure to read ahead and be prepared to take part in the weekly discussions.

Group Study

The lessons in this study guide are suitable for Sunday school classes, small-group studies, elective Bible studies, or home Bible study groups. Each person in the group should have his or her own study guide. You may wish to complete the study guide lesson as homework prior to the meeting of the group and then use the meeting time to discuss the lesson. If you are a group leader, refer to the guide at the back of this book for additional instructions on how to set up and lead your group time.

For Continuing Study

For a complete listing of Dr. Jeremiah's materials for personal and group study, call 1-800-947-1993, go online to www.DavidJeremiah.org, or write to Turning Point, P.O. Box 3838, San Diego, CA 92163.

Dr. Jeremiah's *Turning Point* program is currently heard or viewed around the world on radio, television, and the Internet in English. *Momento Decisivo*, the Spanish translation of Dr. Jeremiah's messages, can be heard on radio in every Spanish speaking country in the world. The television broadcast is also broadcast by satellite throughout the Middle East with Arabic subtitles.

Contact Turning Point for radio and television program times and stations in your area, or visit our website at www.DavidJeremiah.org/ stationlocator.

THE GREAT DISAPPEARANCE

INTRODUCTION

If you ever prepared for a vacation when your children were young, you probably remember the many hours, days, and weeks it took to prepare for your time away from home. Every family member had to have suitable clothing, specific toiletries, and something to keep them occupied during the time on the road, plus maybe a pillow to take a nap. At times, loading the car before a trip was an adventure on its own, plus an instructive lesson on patience! I remember those days well from when Donna and I prepared for vacations when our four children were young. Some of the best family stories include mishaps that occurred getting ready for or during a vacation. Those are precious times to remember.

As the ministry of Turning Point has grown during the past forty years, the number of ministry opportunities has risen too, so it is not uncommon for me to travel several times each month throughout the year. Because Donna and I travel frequently, we know how to prepare for a trip—whether it is for a few days or for a week—because we constantly stay ready for the next adventure on our calendar. We don't wait until the last moment to see if my suit is back from the cleaners or to ask someone to watch our two dogs. We plan—we prepare; we stay ready. We recognized many years ago that preparation is the key to enjoying a stress-free and successful trip.

Staying ready is something that every Christian should also practice each day. The Rapture can happen at any time, so there will be no warning sign in the sky announcing, "Get ready now—He is coming back today!" It doesn't work that way. As you will discover in the lessons that follow, there is no barrier to Christ returning for His Church in the Rapture at any moment. So for those who wish to be a part of *The Great Disappearance*, now is the time to get ready.

Sadly, as in the early days of the Church, there are many people today who scoff and mock the message of the Gospel. They can't believe that anything will change their lives as they know it—especially something as cataclysmic as millions of people leaving their grave or their workplace to be "caught up" to join the Lord in the sky. They will believe odd conspiracy theories such as Bigfoot or aliens on earth, but they find it difficult to believe that Christ will come to take His Church home with Him. That truth seems unbelievable to them. But it is true whether they believe it or not.

But what about those of us who believe and are eagerly waiting for that Great Day? What are we to do as we wait? It is no time to sit back and wait with our hands folded and our eyes toward the sky. We need to urgently invest our resources, our time, and our witness into sharing the Gospel with those who are lost. The opportunity to help others get ready is now. We are the vehicle that God uses to share His amazing plan of salvation to the lost until He comes.

The Bible tells us no one knows when the Rapture will happen, but one thing is certain—it will happen. And following the departure of the saints, the seven-year Tribulation will begin, a harrowing time for anyone who is left behind. Make it your prayer, your earnest desire, to tell as many people as possible about the loving plan God has designed for them. A plan with a beautiful ending—a home in heaven one day—instead of an eternity without God. *The Great Disappearance* is on God's calendar; make sure you are ready and that those you know and love are ready too!

LESSON 1

A GREAT DAY

1 THESSALONIANS 4:13–18

*Discover the promise we have about that Great Day—
the disappearance of the saints in the Rapture.*

Are you living in anticipation of that Great Day when Christ returns for His Church? Throughout biblical history people have speculated about the timing for this event, but only God knows the exact moment when every follower of Christ, living or deceased, will be caught up from earth and taken to heaven. Upon His return, no one who has confessed Christ as Lord will remain behind. What a Great Day that will be!

OUTLINE

I. The Return
 A. The Sound of the Lord's Command
 B. The Sound of Michael's Voice
 C. The Sound of the Trumpet

II. The Resurrection

III. The Redemption
    A. Our New Bodies Will Be Incapable of Sickness or Death
    B. Our New Bodies Will Be Identical to the Body of the Resurrected Jesus
    C. Our New Bodies Will Be Identifiable by All Who Knew Us on Earth
    D. Our New Bodies Will Be Illumined in Brilliance
    E. Our New Bodies Will Be Infinite in Physical Power
    F. Our New Bodies Will Be Incredibly Suited for Heaven and Eternity

IV. The Rapture

V. The Reunion

OVERVIEW

The world we live in today is troubled and hurting, but the good news is that Jesus Christ is coming back for us. And He's coming back soon. The apostle Paul talked excitedly about this Great Day when he said: "And now the prize awaits me—the crown of righteousness, which the Lord, the righteous Judge, will give me on the day of his return. And the prize is not just for me but for all who eagerly look forward to his appearing" (2 Timothy 4:8 NLT).

There's a Great Day that's coming—the day of the Rapture. The exact date is already circled on God's calendar; the year, month, day, hour, minute, and second are locked into the program of God for our planet. The Rapture is an imminent event in the future when all of us, living or deceased, who have put our trust in Christ for salvation and eternal life, will be suddenly caught up from this earth into the heavens. We will be reunited with loved ones who have preceded us in death. And we will be met by the Lord Himself who will usher us into heaven to live forever with Him in perfect fellowship.

The major truth concerning this coming event is found in John 14; 1 Corinthians 15; and 1 Thessalonians 4. John 14 presents our Lord's statement about the many mansions in heaven. First Corinthians 15 is the great Resurrection Chapter. But the chapter that outlines what's going to happen in the Rapture in the very best way is 1 Thessalonians 4.

As we look at the events surrounding the Rapture, there are five significant outcomes—the return, the resurrection, the redemption, the Rapture, and the reunion.

The Return

"For the Lord Himself will descend from heaven with a shout, with the voice of an archangel, and with the trumpet of God. And the dead in Christ will rise first" (1 Thessalonians 4:16). The return of the Lord at the Rapture will be announced by three spectacular sounds.

The Sound of the Lord's Command

The first sound is "the Lord Himself will descend from heaven with a shout" (1 Thessalonians 4:16). The Greek word used to describe the Lord's "shout" is a word that was used to describe a commander coming out of his tent and issuing a command to his followers.

At His return Jesus will shout, "Come forth!" He will call forth believers in graves around the world, and all those tombs will be emptied as the dead in Christ go to be with Jesus.

The Sound of Michael's Voice

The second sound is the sound of Michael's voice. First Thessalonians 4:16 says, "With the voice of an archangel." Michael, the only archangel mentioned in the Bible, will lend his voice to the Rapture.

The Sound of the Trumpet

The third sound is the sound of the trumpet—"with the trumpet of God" (1 Thessalonians 4:16). First Corinthians 15:52 calls it "the last trumpet." The trumpet blast will surround the earth like an echo chamber, reverberating into the soul of every ascending Christian.

The Resurrection

In 1 Thessalonians 4:15–16, we read: "We who are alive and remain until the coming of the Lord will by no means precede those who are asleep. . . . And the dead in Christ will rise first."

When the Lord descends from heaven, He will begin by summoning to Himself those who are asleep. Paul's terminology, "are asleep," is New Testament language which identifies Christians who have died. The following instances from Scripture illustrate this application.

- John 11:11—"These things He said, and after that He said to them, 'Our friend Lazarus sleeps, but I go that I may wake him up.'"
- Acts 7:60—"Then [Stephen] knelt down and cried out with a loud voice, 'Lord, do not charge them with this sin.' And when he had said this, he fell asleep."
- Acts 13:36—"For David, after he had served his own generation by the will of God, fell asleep, was buried with his fathers."

The concept of death in the New Testament is emphasized in a word that early Christians adopted for burying places of their loved ones. It was the Greek term *koimeterion* which means "a rest house for strangers, a sleeping place." It is the word from which we get our English word *cemetery*.

When Christians die, it is as if they are slumbering peacefully in a place of rest, ready to be awakened at the return of the Lord. The words Paul used have great import, for they convey the Christian concept of death, which is not a tragic finality but a temporary sleep.

The Thessalonian believers understood that Jesus was going to come and get them, but they didn't know what was going to happen to their loved ones who had preceded them in death. Would they be left behind? Jesus essentially said, "No, I don't want you to be ignorant about that. I have a plan for that. They will not be left behind; they will precede you in the Rapture." The Rapture is initially for the saved whose bodies are resting in cemeteries.

The Redemption

"So also is the resurrection of the dead. The body is sown in corruption, it is raised in incorruption. It is sown in dishonor, it is raised in glory. It is sown in weakness, it is raised in power. It is sown a natural body, it is raised a spiritual body. There is a natural body, and there is a spiritual body" (1 Corinthians 15:42–44).

At some point in the future, you are going to get an upgrade on your body. The Rapture is going to spark a resurrection renaissance across the globe. And Christians who died will live again—not only spiritually but also physically. The bodies of believers buried in the ground will come out of the ground. They will be raised up.

And those bodies will be transformed in many profound ways. Assuming that you and I pass away before the Rapture, our resurrected bodies on that day will be the same in essence. We will still be humans; you will be you; I will be me. But the resurrection body that emerges will be superior to the old body that you inhabit right now. These words apply not only to those who will be resurrected at the Rapture but also to those who are alive when the Rapture happens.

Our New Bodies Will Be Incapable of Sickness or Death

Our present bodies wear out and grow old. But our resurrection bodies will have no capacity for deterioration or decay. Your new body will be designed for eternity. It will not be subject to accident, disease, aging, or death.

Our New Bodies Will Be Identical to the Body of the Resurrected Jesus

Your new body will be identical to the body of the resurrected Jesus. Philippians 3:20–21 says, "For our citizenship is in heaven, from which we also eagerly wait for the Savior, the Lord Jesus Christ, who will transform our lowly body that it may be conformed to His glorious body, according to the working by which He is able even to subdue all things to Himself."

The Bible tells us that when we are resurrected from the grave or when we are caught up to be with the Lord in the Rapture, we will get bodies that are just like the body Jesus had when He was resurrected. Jesus' body was tangible and touchable, and our new bodies will be like His.

During His post-resurrection appearances, on two occasions Jesus ate with His disciples (see Luke 24; John 21), and He was also able to be touched physically. In John 20:27, Jesus said to Thomas, "Reach your finger here, and look at My hands; and reach your hand here, and put it into My side."

Our New Bodies Will Be Identifiable by All Who Knew Us on Earth

Some people wonder, "Will people know me in my new body?" The Bible is very clear. We will be known as we are known.

After the Resurrection, Jesus knew His disciples, and they knew Him. They recognized the glorified Jesus as the very same One they had known before His death. They were so convinced of the identity of the Lord Jesus Christ in His risen body that they all went to their death proclaiming the reality of the Resurrection.

When Moses and Elijah appeared on the Mount of Transfiguration, the disciples instinctively recognized them both. And when Jesus describes heaven in Matthew 8, He says, "And I say to you that many will come from east and west, and sit down with Abraham, Isaac, and Jacob in the kingdom of heaven" (verse 11).

You're going to remember people, and they're going to remember you.

Our New Bodies Will Be Illumined in Brilliance

When you get to heaven in your new body, you will be illumined in brilliance. In Revelation 21 we're told that in the New Jerusalem a light will emanate from Jesus that will light up the whole city. Matthew 13:43 says, "The righteous will shine forth as the sun in the kingdom of their Father." We're going to shine like the stars.

Our New Bodies Will Be Infinite in Physical Power

Paul said we're buried in weakness but raised in strength and in power (see 1 Corinthians 15:43). When we come out of the grave in a body like Jesus', we'll have so much energy we'll think a lightning bolt has supercharged us. Our resurrection bodies will be incredible, capable of extraordinary functions.

After His resurrection, Jesus could enter sealed rooms without going through the door. John 20:19 says, "Then, the same day at evening, being the first day of the week, when the doors were shut where the disciples were assembled, for fear of the Jews, Jesus came and stood in the midst, and said to them, 'Peace be with you.'"

If the glorified body of Christ could pass through walls and travel by impulses and thought, perhaps it will be true for us as well.

Our New Bodies Will Be Incredibly Suited for Heaven and Eternity

Our bodies now are suited for earth, but our spiritual bodies will be suited for life in heaven and for eternity. Our bodies today have limitations. Heaven and eternity are limitless.

That is the hope we cling to as followers of Jesus. The Rapture assures us that death is not the end of life; it's the beginning of a new existence in our new, perfect, glorious bodies. We're going to heaven someday, and we're going to be there in a way that we can enjoy it.

The Rapture

In 1 Thessalonians 4:17, we learn, "[They] who are alive and remain shall be caught up together with them in the clouds to meet the Lord in the air." "Caught up" is the word *raptura* from the Latin language; this is where we get the word *rapture*.

In a nanosecond, the Lord will call all believers to Himself. We will simply vanish from the earth. No one who has confessed Christ as Lord will be left behind. One day, every Christian on planet Earth is going to be gone.

Husbands will be separated from their wives, wives from their husbands, children from their parents, neighbors from neighbors. One of the reasons I believe that there will be turmoil after the Rapture is that the Holy Spirit who inhabits all believers will be taken out of the world. The Restrainer will be gone. There will be nothing to hold back evil because the Holy Spirit will no longer be present. Everybody on this earth who is a Christian will be gone in a moment.

The Reunion

"Then we who are alive and remain shall be caught up together with them in the clouds to meet the Lord in the air. And thus we shall always be with the Lord" (1 Thessalonians 4:17). At this moment of reunion, the dead will come out of the grave, and their spirits will reenter their bodies. That is the first reunion.

After the dead in Christ are resurrected, all of us who are alive and remain will join them—that is the second reunion. And the final reunion will be when the risen dead and the raptured saints join with Jesus in a glorious reunion in heaven.

"And thus," says the Scripture, "we shall always be with the Lord" (1 Thessalonians 4:17). Is it any wonder that at the end of this passage

Paul said, "Therefore comfort one another with these words" (verse 18)? That's why Christians don't sorrow as the world sorrows when we lose a loved one. When a loved one goes before us and knows Christ as their Savior, we have the assurance that there will be a reunion one day in heaven. There is tremendous comfort in that knowledge.

Are you ready for that Great Day? Be sure to make your reservation and be a part of the glorious reunion in the sky when Jesus returns.

APPLICATION

Personal Questions

1. At the moment of Christ's return, what three sounds will be heard?

2. What is the definition for the Greek word *koimeterion*?

3. Read 1 Thessalonians 4:15–16. For the Christian, how do these verses help us view the concept of death and our resurrection?

4. According to Scripture, what are the six descriptive characteristics of our resurrected bodies?

5. Read 1 Thessalonians 4:17. Describe what might be occurring here on earth after we are caught up to meet the Lord in the air.

6. The reunion is the final event in the Rapture. List the three types of reunions that will occur at that time.

Group Questions

1. As a group, discuss what the Great Day means for each of you and how living in anticipation of Christ's return will affect your daily activities.

2. What assurance does the following verse give to you? "And now the prize awaits me—the crown of righteousness, which the Lord, the righteous Judge, will give me on the day of his return" (2 Timothy 4:8 NLT).

3. Discuss the three sounds that will be heard upon Christ's return (see 1 Thessalonians 4:16).

4. Read 1 Corinthians 15:42–44 as a group and then discuss the six character-istics of our resurrected bodies that are found throughout Scripture.

5. Read 1 Thessalonians 4:17. As a group, discuss and describe what you believe will be happening here on earth as the Church is caught up in the sky with the Lord.

6. The reunion is the final event in the Rapture. List and discuss the three types of reunions that will occur at that time.

DID YOU KNOW?

Have you ever forgotten to send an RSVP to an important event? The term originated in France and is a shorthand for *répondez s'il vous plaît*—which translates to: "respond if you please." It became part of the English vernac-ular in 1845. For formal events like weddings, a response is still expected. But in less formal situations today, the RSVP is being misused—many peo-ple believe it means to respond if you are coming, but if you don't plan to attend, no response is necessary. This leaves the person who sent the invitation in a quandary—did the person receive the invitation or are they simply not coming? If you haven't settled that question with God, tell Him whether you will be joining in the *Great Disappearance*—return your RSVP.

LESSON 2

THE NOAH FACTOR

MATTHEW 24:36–44

In this lesson we see the similarities between
"as in the days of Noah" and our lives today.

In a small Dutch town along the Maas River sits a reproduction of the vessel God commanded Noah to construct in the book of Genesis. Built by carpenter and creationist Johan Huibers in 2012, "Johan's Ark" is 390 feet long and 75 feet tall. This massive vessel is a replica of Noah's ark—featuring animal stalls, model animals, feeding troughs, and more—plus it even floats! Why did Johan Huibers build his ark? He said, "I wanted children to come here and feel the texture of the wood, see the nails and see that what is written in the book is true . . . . I wanted to spread God's Word in the Netherlands." Specifically, Huibers wants people to recognize the dangers of our current age. "I believe we are living in the end of times," he says. "We're not conscious of it. People never are."[1]

OUTLINE

    I. A Cavalier Generation

    II. A Careless Generation

III. A Corrupt Generation

IV. A "Caught Off Guard" Generation

OVERVIEW

Matthew 24:37 says, "But as the days of Noah were, so also will the coming of the Son of Man be." Jesus did not promise to return when the world conditions resembled the days of Abraham or the days of Daniel or the days of Paul. Jesus said He will come again during a period of history resembling the days of Noah.

A Cavalier Generation

Jesus spoke of this parallel when He said, "For as in the days before the flood, they were eating and drinking, marrying and giving in marriage, until the day that Noah entered the ark, and did not know until the flood came and took them all away, so also will the coming of the Son of Man be" (Matthew 24:38–39).

When you read that a generation is *cavalier*, it indicates a dismissive attitude that ignores prevailing warning signs. Notice that in this passage Jesus was not talking about people doing bad things. He was talking about people doing normal things and taking life as it came.

Noah preached to his generation about salvation from the coming Flood for 120 years! He was faithful to tell them the way of salvation, but they would not listen. Rather than turning to God in repentance, they filled their lives with eating, drinking, and enjoying their own pursuits.

Jesus said the days before the Rapture will be like that too. People will continue to live as they have always lived despite cataclysmic warnings and predictions. They will focus on the present and its pleasures. They will not give any thought to the possibility that the prophets of the Bible and Noah might be right.

In Luke's account of Noah, he added another story right next to it. He said: "Likewise as it was also in the days of Lot: They ate, they drank, they bought, they sold, they planted, they built; but on the day that Lot went out of Sodom it rained fire and brimstone from heaven and destroyed them all. Even so will it be in the day when the Son of Man is revealed" (Luke 17:28–30).

Dr. John Hart wrote, "The most transparent meaning of the 'days of Noah' illustration . . . is that, just as normal but unsuspecting lifestyles existed prior to the great judgment of the flood, so too normal but unsuspecting lifestyles will exist prior to . . . the rapture of the church."[2]

We see the evidence of the cavalier lifestyles in the declining attendance in churches in America and around the world. The attitude about church attendance reflects the cavalier attitude about life in the world today.

A Careless Generation

In Hebrews 11 we learn more about the days of Noah. In listing the heroes of the faith, the author of Hebrews said, "By faith Noah, being divinely warned of things not yet seen, moved with godly fear, prepared an ark for the saving of his household, by which he condemned the world and became heir of the righteousness which is according to faith" (verse 7).

When God spoke to Noah, this man of faith believed Him, and he was "moved with godly fear." Noah was concerned for his family, his neighbors, and the people around him. Everyone else seemed to be careless about others, but Noah cared. He must have cared a lot to take on the assignment to build something so massive—to care for not only the eight souls in his family but also for the people whom he hoped would join them and be saved from destruction. But only eight souls went into that ark in the book of Genesis. It illustrates how easy it is at times to ignore the warnings people give us about the dangers that are ahead.

So many people are ignoring the spiritual warning signs because they feel they're bulletproof. It's inconceivable to them that anything cataclysmic could ever happen to them.

Peter must have been thinking about Jesus' words on the Mount of Olives when he wrote: "Scoffers will come in the last days, walking according to their own lusts, and saying, 'Where is the promise of His coming? For since the fathers fell asleep, all things continue as they were from the beginning of creation.' For this they willfully forget: that by the word of God the heavens were of old, and the earth standing out of water and in the water, by which the world that then existed perished, being flooded with water" (2 Peter 3:3–6).

Peter said the scoffers will mock and joke as they pursue their own godless interests, but even as they do that, they will forget this happened before. For 120 years people listened to Noah preach—they mocked and scoffed too but didn't listen to the message he was proclaiming. But the day came. And the door closed. And the Flood started.

A Corrupt Generation

Genesis 6:11–12 says this about the time of Noah: "The earth also was corrupt before God, and the earth was filled with violence. So God looked upon the earth, and indeed it was corrupt; for all flesh had corrupted their way on the earth."

The word "corrupt" is in that passage three times. And earlier Genesis 6:5 says, "The wickedness of man was great in the earth, and . . . every intent of the thoughts of his heart was only evil continually."

First, it was a great wickedness. This speaks of the intensity of it. It was full-grown with no regard for right or for God. Second, it affected every intent of man's heart and "every intent of the thoughts of his heart." Third, man was "only evil." If man had a choice between right and wrong, he chose the wrong. Finally, he was "only evil continually." He lived in sin all the time.

It was not just that man's thoughts were evil but also that he intended his thoughts to be evil. And it wasn't just that some of his thoughts were evil but that all of his thoughts were evil. And it wasn't that his thoughts were good sometimes and evil sometimes, but that his thoughts were evil all the time.

Nowhere in the pages of the Bible is there a more complete definition of the doctrine of total depravity. "To most persons 'total' means 'utterly,' and utter depravity would mean that people are as bad as they can possibly be. That is not true, of course. Given the finite circumstances of our lives, civil laws, and various social and religious restraints, each of us could undoubtedly be much worse than we are. What total depravity is meant to convey is the idea that sin has affected the whole person down to the very core or root of his or her being."[3]

Sin touches every aspect of life. In Noah's day, people had vile, evil imaginations. That hasn't changed. Now we have the technology to put all these images, even ones worse than you or I could imagine, on screens and instantly transport them to a billion depraved minds with a click of a button.

The wickedness of man affected his *will*. He was evil because he wanted to be evil. It affected his *thoughts*—his thoughts refer to his mind and demonstrate that his intellect was polluted by sin. It affected his *heart*—everything he did, and everything he was, was touched by sin.

The passage also speaks of the violence of Noah's day. Discord, chaos, and violence always come from uncontrolled wickedness. Where there is no righteousness, there will be wickedness. Genesis 6:11 reminds us, "The earth was filled with violence." As in the days of Noah, we see murderous assaults on people across the world. We live in a depraved time where wickedness is rampant.

Is it any wonder that God's heart was grieved as He looked down from His heavenly vantage point and decided to begin anew on earth?

A "Caught Off Guard" Generation

And finally, their generation was "caught off guard." Matthew 24:39 says, "And [they] did not know until the flood came and took them all away, so also will the coming of the Son of Man be."

Jesus also says in Matthew 24: "As the days of Noah were, so also will the coming of the Son of Man be . . . . Then two men will be in the field: one will be taken and the other left. Two women will be grinding at the mill: one will be taken and the other left" (verses 37, 40–41).

The word "taken" is the Greek word *paralambano,* and just two days later Jesus used that word in the Upper Room. He told His disciples, "If I go and prepare a place for you, I will come again, and receive you unto myself" (John 14:3 KJV). The word "receive" is the word *paralambano,* "to take to oneself."

In other words, Jesus said that during times resembling those of Noah He would return and some people would be "taken" or "received." And two days later He repeated the point to His disciples: I will receive you . . . I will take you unto Myself.

I've read other explanations for our Lord's words about some being taken and some left, but I can't get away from the plain and straightforward implication of the Rapture. If these verses were talking about the Second Coming of Christ at the end of the Tribulation or about people being taken away in the judgments of the Tribulation, why would life be going on as usual—eating, drinking, marrying, and giving in marriage, living carelessly and with a cavalier attitude?

People are going to be caught off guard! Look at this entire passage and notice the first and last sentences:

> But of that day and hour no one knows, not even the angels of heaven, but My Father only. But as the days of Noah were, so also will the coming of the Son of Man be. For as in the days before the flood, they were eating and drinking, marrying and giving in marriage, until the day that Noah entered the ark, and did not know until the flood came and took them all away, so also will the coming of the Son of Man be. Then two men will be in the field: one will be taken and the other left. Two women will be grinding at the mill: one will be taken and the other left. Watch therefore, for you do not know what hour your Lord is coming (Matthew 24:36–42).

Jesus began the passage telling us that no one knows the day or the hour. He ends on the same note by telling us we do not know what hour the Lord is coming. Jesus said to watch and be ready. Right now, the door to salvation is wide open—just like the door of the ark was wide open for 120 years while a man faithfully preached repentance and told the people what they needed to do.

One of the interesting things about the original ark was that it only had one door. Jesus said, "I am the door" (John 10:7). If you want to get into the ark of salvation, you have to come through Jesus Christ. There's one door and one way to safety, and that's through Christ. If you wait and you don't ask Jesus Christ to come into your life and enter the ark of salvation, you will be left outside, as were the people in Noah's day when the Flood came.

Without Christ, you're living in the days of Noah—cavalier, careless, corrupt, about to be caught by surprise. At any moment, the door will swing shut, the Lord will come for His Church, and you will be left behind.

The Gospel invitation that was given to Noah was the word "come." "Come into the ark, you and all your household, because I have seen that you are righteous before Me in this generation" (Genesis 7:1). This is the first mention of this familiar word in the Bible. One of the last times it is mentioned is in Revelation 22:17: "And the Spirit and the bride say, 'Come!' . . . And let him who thirsts come. Whoever desires, let him take the water of life freely." It is the offer of salvation for any who will come and escape the judgment that will fall on this earth. The final mention of "come" is in Revelation 22:20, "Come, Lord Jesus!" Don't miss the opportunity to enter the safety of the ark of God's love. He is waiting for you to "Come"!

APPLICATION

Personal Questions

1. Read Matthew 24:37–39. Write down the four ways that the times we are living in are like the days of Noah.

2. In what way does being cavalier about the future affect the downward spiral of church attendance found in Western cultures?

3. How does the normalcy of routine become a hindrance to listening to the voice of God?

4. What characteristic made Noah stand firm even as he was being mocked and ridiculed?

5. How does carelessness play a role in rejecting God's plan for His children? What kept Noah from falling prey to peer pressure?

6. The world today is filled with corruption as it was in Noah's day. What three aspects of man are corrupted by wickedness?

7. How is the total depravity of man seen in our world today?

8. Even though Noah spent 120 years building the ark, the culture of his day was caught off guard when the door of the ark closed. How is that a foreshadowing of what will happen one day to the world we live in?

9. Read John 14:3. What does this verse mean to you in light of the coming Rapture?

Group Questions

1. Read Matthew 24:38 together. Examine each of the four main points in this lesson, and discuss ways that you see cavalier, careless, corrupt, and "caught off guard" generations in your community, state, and the world today.

2. If comfortable, share possible actions or steps you can employ to avoid being cavalier or careless in your walk with God.

3. What lesson(s) can you learn from Noah's perseverance in building the ark even as he was mocked and ridiculed by the people he was hoping to save along with his family one day?

4. Write down and discuss the three ways that wickedness corrupts a person.

5. As a group discuss things in your life that could cause you to be careless in your walk with God and in your expectation of His return.

6. It is easy to observe how our culture is being corrupted by the things we see, do, allow, and watch. Discuss ways that you as a group can reflect the love of God to those who are ensnared by the corruption and wickedness that is pervasive in our world today.

DID YOU KNOW?

According to recent Gallup studies, only 20 percent of Americans attend church every week, down from 32 percent attending church regularly in 2000. Regular church attendance has steadily declined since the turn of the century, and pandemic closures only escalated that decline. Before the pandemic, "two-thirds of all churches had an attendance of around 125. Now 2 in 3 churches are at less than 100 in attendance, with nearly 1 in 3 churches below 50." The most shocking statistic is that 57 percent of Americans seldom or never attend church.[4] As in the days of Noah, people are pursuing their daily activities and interests rather than the worship of Almighty God.

Notes
1. Cnaan Liphshiz, "Dutch Christian Boat Maker Aims to Sail His Exact Replica of Noah's Ark to Israel," *The Times of Israel*, November 24, 2018, https://www.timesofisrael.com/dutch-christian-boatmaker-to-sail-his-life-size-replica-of-noahs-ark-to-israel/.
2. John Hart, ed., *Evidence for the Rapture* (Chicago, IL: Moody Publishers, 2015), 56–57.
3. James Montgomery Boice and Philip Graham Ryken, *The Doctrines of Grace* (Wheaton, IL: Crossway, 2002), 70–71.
4. "The State of Church Attendance: Trends and Statistics [2023]," Churchtrac, https://www.churchtrac.com/articles/the-state-of-church-attendance-trends-and-statistics-2023.

IF WE DIE

PSALM 23

*In this lesson we discover that death,
for the Christian, is nothing to fear.*

Death is one of those subjects most people tend to avoid talking about. In fact, if they're honest, most people are afraid of death and what lies on "the other side." Without the Bible's assurances, fear of death is understandable. But for the Christian, death is a welcome transition to glory.

OUTLINE

I. **The Fact of Death**

II. **The Faces of Death**
   A. Physical Death
   B. Spiritual Death
   C. Second Death

III. **The Fear of Death**
   A. The Prince of Death Has Been Defeated
   B. The Power of Death Has Been Destroyed

    C. The Process of Death Has Been Described
    D. The Picture of Death Has Been Developed

OVERVIEW

Most people don't even like to talk about it or use the word *death*. But the most real book in the world, the Bible, doesn't shy away from the subject of death—and neither should we. After all, it's something that one hundred percent of human beings will experience (except those alive at the moment of the Rapture, of course).

The Fact of Death

The fact of death makes it a mandatory subject for consideration regardless of how we feel about it. But the truth is, we don't need to fear death. By looking at what the Bible says on the subject, we can dispel the aura of fear that surrounds the subject of death. Even for many Christians, in spite of their confidence in having eternal life, death is a subject to be avoided. But it shouldn't be, given what it represents for the Christian.

The Faces of Death

Death has three faces, and the key word for each is *separation*. That's really what death is—a separation that happens in three dimensions.

Physical Death

The soul and spirit are separated from the body when we die physically. Our body remains on earth while the soul and spirit migrate into the presence of God or to another place where God is not present. (I'm speaking in the most general terms simply to illustrate the notion of separation.)

For example, James 2:26 says that "the body without the spirit is dead." It is the immaterial part of man that animates, or gives life to, the material part of man (see Genesis 2:7). When the immaterial part separates from the material part, the material part dies. Genesis 35:18 speaks of Rachel's "soul . . .

departing" when she died. Solomon wrote about the spirit of man return-ing "to God who gave it" (Ecclesiastes 12:7).

We are more familiar with what happens to the body at the time of death because our experience has ingrained that idea in our understand-ing: The body is buried. Because we don't see what happens to the spirit and soul, we have less of a sense of their departure. But the Bible is clear on what happens—the immaterial part of man is separated from the physical part of man at death.

Spiritual Death

When we talk about spiritual death, we mean the separation of the spirit from God. Said another way, we were all born dead because we were sep-arated from God. When Adam sinned and died spiritually, his spiritual death was transmitted to the entire human race so that all were born dead in sin: "Therefore, just as through [Adam] sin entered the world, and death through sin, and thus death spread to all men, because all sinned" (Romans 5:12). Further, "The wages of sin is death" (Romans 6:23).

Every human being ever born (with the exception of Jesus of Nazareth because of His sinless conception by the Holy Spirit) has been born separated spiritually from God. That is at the heart of the Gospel—man-kind's need to be spiritually "born again" and united with God rather than separated from Him.

Second Death

While spiritual death carries with it the potential of bridging one's sepa-ration from God by being born again through faith in Christ, the second death is much more ominous. The second death is the eternal separation of man from God. In the vision of end time events seen by the apostle John in his vision, he called being "cast into the lake of fire" the "second death." And who will experience this second, eternal death? "Anyone not found written in the Book of Life" (Revelation 20:14–15).

Think of the three faces of death this way: If you have been born only once, you will have to die twice. But if you have been born twice, you will only have to die once.

Here's the explanation: If you have only been born once (at your phys-ical birth), you will have to die twice (physically and spiritually). But if you have been born twice (once physically, then born again through faith in Christ), you will only have to die once (physically). (Again, those alive when the Rapture occurs won't even die once!)

Jesus said something similar when His friend Lazarus died: "Jesus said to her, 'I am the resurrection and the life. He who believes in Me, though he may die, he shall live. And whoever lives and believes in Me shall never die. Do you believe this?' " (John 11:25–26).

So if you want to live forever with God, you must be born twice: physically and then spiritually through faith in Christ. That's why Jesus said, "Most assuredly, I say to you, unless one is born again, he cannot see the kingdom of God" (John 3:3).

The Fear of Death

If more people in this world understood the three faces of death—especially the last one, the second death—they might be even more afraid of death than they already are. But for a Christian the story is different. The Christian has no need to fear any of the three faces of death—for the following four reasons.

The Prince of Death Has Been Defeated

First, the prince of death has been destroyed. Jesus became flesh and blood so that "through death He might destroy him who had the power of death, that is, the devil, and release those who through fear of death were all their lifetime subject to bondage" (Hebrews 2:14–15).

What a powerful statement! Jesus came into the world to liberate all of humanity from the fear of death. No one needs to live in bondage to such a fear.

Christ's death must have seemed to Satan like the ultimate victory. But when Christ stepped forth from the tomb, thereby taking the sting out of death, Satan was defeated. Satan's fate was sealed. Yes, he is still active in this world, but he knows the fear of death has been removed from his toolbox.

I read about a couple in Tennessee who were sitting in their breakfast nook one morning, with their little dog lying on a bench right in front of the bay window. Suddenly, a huge "thump" scared the dog off the bench. A hawk had seen the little dog and flown down to nab it and crashed directly into the glass in the bay window. The dog was fine, and the hawk regained its composure and flew off.

In a similar way, we are protected from Satan's talons by the death and resurrection of Christ. Satan, the prince of death, has been defeated.

The Power of Death Has Been Destroyed

It stands to reason that if the prince of death has been defeated, then the power of death has been destroyed. And it has: " 'O Death, where is your sting? O Hades, where is your victory?' The sting of death is sin, and the strength of sin is the law. But thanks be to God, who gives us the victory through our Lord Jesus Christ" (1 Corinthians 15:55-57). In eternity there will be no death at all. It, along with sorrow, crying, pain, and tears, will have "passed away" (Revelation 21:4).

The Process of Death Has Been Described

The first two truths about the prince and power of death are good reasons not to fear death. But for added comfort we can read how the Bible describes death. There are lots of books about people claiming to have had an ADE—an after-death experience in which they visit heaven and come back to tell about it. Thankfully, we have a more authoritative source on which to depend.

The source is a parable Jesus told about two men who died—one rich and the other poor. The rich man used his wealth for his own pleasure; the poor man, named Lazarus, used to search for crumbs to eat outside the rich man's gate. The rich man possessed something he couldn't keep— his life—while the poor man possessed something he couldn't lose—love for God. Both men died and went to different places. The poor man was carried by angels to the bosom of Abraham—a metaphor for eternal bliss (see Luke 16:19-31).

Growing up, I used to hear people refer to angels taking a person to heaven at the moment of death, and I thought it was just an image, something to make them feel better. Until, that is, I read this parable and understood that Jesus portrayed that very experience in His parable. Parables use truths to form the basis of stories to illustrate a lesson. In this parable, the lesson is about the different destinations of Lazarus and the rich man. But one of the truths employed is that angels are sent from heaven to escort God's people to His presence when those people die.

That should be a great comfort to every Christian, another reason to have no fear of the experience of death. Escorted by angels—as they say, "What a way to go!"

The Picture of Death Has Been Developed

One of the most famous verses from one of the most famous passages in all the Bible is the foundation for this final truth: "Yea, though I walk through the valley of the shadow of death, I will fear no evil; for You are with me; Your rod and Your staff, they comfort me" (Psalm 23:4).

When Peter Marshall, the chaplain of the U.S. Senate, was speaking to Annapolis cadets in a chapel service in 1941, he told them a story of a little boy who had a terminal disease. The boy asked his mother if it hurt to die. Her answer was to remind him of how sometimes he would fall asleep in his parents' bed but wake up in his own bed the next morning. Either she or the boy's father would carry the little one gently to his own bed without him waking up. That, she told him, is what death is like—going to sleep on earth and waking up in heaven.

Psalm 23:4 gives us a similar picture of the transition from life on earth to life in heaven.

- **Death Is a Journey, Not a Destination** ("Through the valley"). The key word is "through." Death is not the destination; it is not a place. Rather, death is a brief journey, a transition, from earth to heaven. As my friend Robert Morgan has expressed in his book *The Lord Is My Shepherd*, death is a valley "which means it has an opening on both ends. . . . Valleys don't go on forever."[1] Rather than a place to go to, death is something you go *through* and come out in a new place. Death means being "absent from the body and to be present with the Lord" (2 Corinthians 5:8). Someone has said that death is an exit and heaven is an entrance, one opening as the other closes. There is nothing to fear about a journey when the Lord is our shepherd through it.

- **Death Is a Shadow, Not a Reality** ("The valley of the shadow"). Psalm 23:4 doesn't say we pass through the "valley of death" but through the "valley of the shadow of death." For the Christian, death is just a shadow. It can appear menacing but is harmless. Shadows never hurt anyone. One of my daily chores as a young boy was to take the garbage out every night and empty it in the trash can. I had to pass through a dark garage lighted by only a single light bulb that cast all sorts of eerie shadows. I played in that garage during the day, but at night the shadows made it a scary place—harmless, but scary for a little boy. Death can seem scary, but it's only a shadow, nothing for the Christian to fear.

- **Death Is Lonely, but You Are Never Alone** ("You are with me"). A beautiful thing happens in Psalm 23. In the first three verses, David is talking *about* God: He makes me; He leads me; He restores; He leads. But in verse 4 David begins talking *to* God: You are with me; Your rod and Your staff; You prepare a table; You anoint my head. Right when he realizes he's in the valley of the shadow of death, David begins talking directly to God. It's his way of saying that God is right there with him as he goes through the valley. David knows he is not alone.

If you are a Christian—God's child through faith in Christ—then the promises of Scripture about death belong to you. Anticipate the end of life with joy instead of fear!

APPLICATION

Personal Questions

1. How would you describe your feelings about your own death one day?

a. If you are a Christian, are your feelings consistent with the biblical assurances you read in this lesson? (Do your head and your emotions agree about death?)

b. What did you learn in this lesson about death that provided comfort, surprise, or knowledge?

c. How might you use the content of this lesson when talking with a non-Christian about the subject of death?

2. Read 1 John 5:11–13.

a. What is the source of eternal life (see verse 11)?

b. How does verse 12 make it very clear as to who will never die and who will experience the second death?

c. Why did John say he wrote his first epistle (see verse 13)?

d. How do you know that you have eternal life—that you do not need to ever fear death?

3. What four reasons does this lesson give as to why we, as Christians, shouldn't fear death? How can you use each as an encouragement when the fear of death creeps into your life?

Group Questions

1. With your group, explain the analogy the apostle James makes between the physical body and faith. How is the human spirit like good works (see James 2:26)?

2. How did God animate Adam in the Garden of Eden (see Genesis 2:7)?

   a. How is that process reversed when a person dies?

   b. What do you think—does the spirit of man leave when the body dies or does the body die when the spirit leaves?

   c. Which is the cause of physical death—the body expiring or the spirit leaving the body (see Revelation 11:11)?

3. The second death affects only those whose names are missing from the Book of Life. When is that book first mentioned and under what circumstances (see Exodus 32:30–35)?

a. How does Paul use the Book of Life with reference to Christians in Philippians 4:3?

b. Who will worship the Antichrist during the Tribulation (see Revelation 13:8)?

c. What confidence do you have that your name is written in the Lamb's Book of Life (see Revelation 21:22–27)? If you're comfortable, share with the group as an encouragement to one another.

DID YOU KNOW?

The Population Reference Bureau in Washington, D.C., estimates that, as of 2022, there have been approximately 117 billion people who have lived on planet Earth.[2] Given that there are around 8 billion people alive today, that means 109 billion people have died already. Put another way, approximately 14 people have died for every 1 person alive today. Hundreds of thousands of people die in the world each day. Physical death is not an exclusive club—it is common to all mankind—but we can escape spiritual death through the sacrifice of the Lamb of God.

Notes
1. Robert J. Morgan, *The Lord Is My Shepherd* (New York: Howard Books, 2013), 116–117.
2. Toshiko Kaneda and Carl Haub, "How Many People Have Ever Lived on Earth?" *Population Reference Bureau*, November 15, 2022, https://www.prb.org/articles/how-many-people-have-ever-lived-on-earth.

WILL CHILDREN BE RAPTURED?

2 SAMUEL 12:14–23

*In this lesson we discuss God's relationship
with children and their future with Him.*

Saying a final goodbye to a loved one is always difficult, but what if that loved one is an infant who never breathed their first breath or a toddler who is taken too soon—what happens to them? Will we ever see them again? In this lesson we will reveal answers to those questions and others as we reflect upon the Father's love and the future He has planned for children.

OUTLINE

I. **The Character of God**

II. **The Condition for Salvation**

III. **The Compassion of the Savior**

IV. **The Child of David**

OVERVIEW

What will happen to young children on the day of the Rapture? Does the Bible offer any clarity for parents and grandparents, any hope for all of us?

Understanding what happens to children when they die is the key to understanding what happens to them should they be living on the earth when the Rapture happens. Scripture gives us four solid reasons for believing that children who die and children who are living when the Rapture occurs will go straight to heaven.

The Character of God

The Bible is full of information about the nature and character of God, His personality, His attributes, and His many descriptive names. Scripture calls Him "Father." He isn't simply a distant force in the universe. He is, as Jesus put it, "Our Father in heaven" (Matthew 6:9).

There's a tender passage describing the Father's love in Deuteronomy which says, "Then I said to you, 'Do not be terrified, or afraid of them. The Lord your God, who goes before you, He will fight for you, according to all He did for you in Egypt before your eyes, and in the wilderness where you saw how the Lord your God carried you, as a man carries his son, in all the way that you went until you came to this place' " (Deuteronomy 1:29–31).

The Bible presents God as a Father who is full of compassion and tenderness and mercy. He carries us through the tough patches like a father carries his son. This is a consistent theme, especially in the Psalms. Psalm 86:15 says, "But You, O Lord, are a God full of compassion, and gracious, longsuffering and abundant in mercy and truth." And Psalm 145:9 says, "The LORD is good to all, and His tender mercies are over all His works."

God is a good God. He is good to all, including children. He knows that little children cannot comprehend the truth of the Gospel, and He loves them deeply.

There are specific incidents in the Old Testament that help us gain an understanding of our Father's love. When the children of Israel were denied entrance into the Promised Land because of the unbelief of the people, the children were not held responsible, and God allowed them to enter. Here you see the principle of God applying His grace to those who cannot believe. God is treating children in a unique manner. "Moreover your little ones and your children, who you say will be victims, who today have no knowledge of good and evil, they shall go in there; to them I will give it, and they shall possess it" (Deuteronomy 1:39). Their parents couldn't go. Their older brothers and sisters couldn't go, but the little children could go. They were not responsible for what had happened.

God's pity on the city of Nineveh was based upon the large number of children who lived in the city who were yet unable to discern right and wrong. He said, "And should I not pity Nineveh, that great city, in which are more than one hundred and twenty thousand persons who cannot discern between their right hand and their left" (Jonah 4:11).

The word *children* appears more than one hundred times in the New Testament, and the Bible teaches that God knows and loves children with special, tender care. Our Heavenly Father provides for children who are not old enough to comprehend the Gospel.

The character of God provides a special grace for those who cannot believe. On several occasions, God refers to these little ones as innocents. Jeremiah 2:34 says, "Also on your skirts is found the blood of the lives of the poor innocents." And Jeremiah 19:4 says, "And have filled this place with the blood of the innocents." Even though we know that everyone is born in sin, children are not responsible in the same way as those whose sins are willful and premeditated, and God understands the difference.

The character of God lays the foundation for the realization that children who cannot understand the Gospel are enveloped within the grace and mercy of our Lord.

The Condition for Salvation

Next, we can understand what happens to children at the Rapture on the condition of salvation. What must a person do to be lost? They must refuse the free offer of God's saving grace.

John MacArthur put it this way: "Little children have no record of unbelief or evil works and therefore, there is no basis for their deserving an eternity apart from God . . . . They are graciously and sovereignly saved by God as part of the atoning work of Jesus Christ."[1]

Isaiah the prophet speaks about such a period in the innocence of the life of a child: "For before the Child shall know to refuse the evil and choose the good" (7:16). In other words, there's a time before a child knows how to refuse evil and to choose good.

The Compassion of the Savior

When we read the stories of Jesus in the Gospels, we discover that our Lord had an incredible love for children, and He demonstrated that love on many occasions. He talked about them every time He had an opportunity. Whenever they were near Him, He had something to say about it. One example is so important that it is recorded by three of the Gospel writers—Matthew, Mark, and Luke. In Matthew 19:13–14, we read, "Then little children were brought to Him that He might put His hands on them and pray, but the disciples rebuked them. But Jesus said, 'Let the little children come to Me, and do not forbid them; for of such is the kingdom of heaven.'"

We also have another passage in Matthew that is as definitive as any verse in the Bible on the eternal love that Jesus has for children. "Even so it is not the will of your Father who is in heaven that one of these little ones should perish" (18:14). The Lord Jesus has compassion for little children and infants and is not willing that even one of them should perish.

I believe, as do all who accept the authority of God's Word, that a child is a person from the moment of conception. Since that is true, all preborn babies who perish, whether through miscarriage, abortion, or tragic accidents, go straight to heaven.

Your little one will be in heaven because of the compassion of Jesus, for they have not yet come to the place where they can understand the truth of the Gospel.

The Child of David

Perhaps the greatest proof of the assurance of children in heaven is found in the Old Testament story about the child of David. There's an incident in the life of David that is fundamental to the question we are answering.

In 2 Samuel 12, David is confronted concerning his adultery with Bathsheba and the murder of her husband Uriah. Among other things,

Nathan told David that the child that he and Bathsheba had brought into the world would be taken away in death.

In 2 Samuel 12:14–23, we read:

"However, because by this deed you have given great occasion to the enemies of the Lord to blaspheme, the child also who is born to you shall surely die." Then Nathan departed to his house. And the Lord struck the child that Uriah's wife bore to David, and it became ill. David therefore pleaded with God for the child, and David fasted and went in and lay all night on the ground. So the elders of his house arose and went to him, to raise him up from the ground. But he would not, nor did he eat food with them. Then on the seventh day it came to pass that the child died. And the servants of David were afraid to tell him that the child was dead. For they said, "Indeed, while the child was alive, we spoke to him, and he would not heed our voice. How can we tell him that the child is dead? He may do some harm!"

When David saw that his servants were whispering, David perceived that the child was dead. Therefore David said to his servants, "Is the child dead?" And they said, "He is dead." So David arose from the ground, washed and anointed himself, and changed his clothes; and he went into the house of the Lord and worshiped. Then he went to his own house; and when he requested, they set food before him, and he ate. Then his servants said to him, "What is this that you have done? You fasted and wept for the child while he was alive, but when the child died, you arose and ate food."

And he said, "While the child was alive, I fasted and wept; for I said, 'Who can tell whether the Lord will be gracious to me, that the child may live?' But now he is dead; why should I fast? Can I bring him back again? I shall go to him, but he shall not return to me."

The last sentence in that passage is arguably the greatest sentence in the Bible about what happens to a child when they die or should the Rapture occur.

David was saying, "I cannot bring him back, but I can go to where he is." David knew that when little ones die or if the Rapture happens before they understand the Gospel, they go to heaven.

Some people will ask, "What is the age of accountability?" In our attempt to bring comfort to those who mourn, we must not deny the truth of God's Word. No one really is truly innocent. Jesus' statements about children being innocents does not mean that they are without sin. It means that they were not responsible for their sin. The Bible teaches that all of us are sinners.

There are no exceptions. All of us are born with a sin nature. Even though we have not yet done anything wrong, our nature is sinful. Every baby needs a Savior just as every adult does. But at what age does a child become responsible for his relationship with God? Is there an age of accountability? Isaiah refers to such a time in the life of a child: "For before the Child shall know to refuse the evil and choose the good" (Isaiah 7:16).

It is important to recognize that the Bible does not make any reference to an age of accountability. It's not there. But there is a time in the life of every child when they understand God's love and when they comprehend what it means to be a sinner.

There comes a time when you truly understand the Gospel. For some children that knowledge comes early. For others it may take more time. The age of accountability is not a chronological measurement; it's a reckoning of spiritual understanding. Before you understand, the Bible protects you under the blood of Christ.

There is another question that often comes up in this setting, and that is the question of how old children will be in heaven. There are differing views about that. Some people believe that when we are in heaven we will all be mature in body, mind, and spirit. And the thought is this, if babies cannot fully enjoy this life, how could we expect them to fully enjoy eternal life with God? One proponent of this view argues that the book of Revelation describes worship in heaven as involving everyone. Therefore, whoever's in heaven will have to be of such an age to be able to participate in the eternal worship of God.

I believe children will be allowed to grow up in heaven. My reasoning on this subject is biblical. We know that right before heaven is the Millennium, the thousand-year reign of Christ. And if you study that period, children are present. In fact, Isaiah 11 says, "And a little child shall lead them . . . . The nursing child shall play by the cobra's hole, and the weaned child shall put his hand in the viper's den" (verses 6, 8).

So when children go to heaven, and I don't have all the information and all the details and all the ramifications of this, it appears that children will grow up in heaven.

If you have experienced the loss of an infant or child my heart goes out to you—the pain is immense—but for the believer, even though we sorrow, we have the blessed assurance of a reunion with that child someday.

God has promised us in His Word that He is caring for the innocent one who dies or who is alive when the Rapture happens. There will be people of all ages coming together and going to heaven on that day—from infants to the aged—our reunion in heaven is assured.

APPLICATION

Personal Questions

1. Read the following verses and then write down what aspect of God's character is seen in how He cares for children.

    a. Deuteronomy 1:29–31

    b. Deuteronomy 1:39

    c. Jonah 4:11

2. How does God's character show that there is a special grace for the innocents who cannot believe?

3. What must a person do to be lost for all eternity?

4. Read Isaiah 7:16. How does this verse help you understand the moral innocence of children?

5. Read Matthew 19:13–14, Mark 10:13–14, and Luke 18:15–16. What do these verses illustrate about Jesus' love for the "little children"?

6. In Matthew 18:14, we read "Even so it is not the will of your Father who is in heaven that one of these little ones should perish." What does this say about Christ's compassion for those who have not had the opportunity to accept Him?

7. Read 2 Samuel 12:14–23. In verse 23, what did David mean when he said, "I shall go to him, but he shall not return to me"?

8. Describe the age of accountability in terms of children understanding the grace and mercy of God for them.

Group Questions

1. Read the following verses together and then discuss the various aspects of God's character as it is displayed in these Scriptures.

    a. Deuteronomy 1:29–31

    b. Deuteronomy 1:39

    c. Jonah 4:11

2. As a group discuss how God's character illustrates that there is a special grace for the innocents who cannot believe like those who have been lost prior to birth or shortly thereafter.

3. Together discuss what is required for a person to be lost for all eternity.

4. Read Matthew 19:13–14, Mark 10:13–14, and Luke 18:15–16. Discuss how these verses illustrate Jesus' love for the "little children."

5. Read 2 Samuel 12:14–23. Discuss the meaning of "I shall go to him, but he shall not return to me" in verse 23. What kind of assurance does that give you regarding the future of little children?

6. Discuss the age of accountability. What does it mean in terms of children understanding the grace and mercy of God for them?

DID YOU KNOW?

Abraham Lincoln is known and respected for his personal strength and integrity as our sixteenth president. But from an early age, his life was filled with sorrow and loss, which no doubt formed his ideas about God and faith in Christ. His mother, Nancy, died when he was nine. And he and his wife, Mary Todd Lincoln, lost one son at the age of three. During their time in the White House, they lost their eleven-year-old son, Willie, to typhoid fever. Upon Willie's death Abraham said, "My poor boy, he was too good for this earth. God has called him home. I know that he is much better off in heaven, but then we loved him so. It is hard, hard to have him die."[2] It is so hard to lose someone we love, but when we know we will see them again one day, we are able to find comfort and peace.

Notes

1. John MacArthur, *Safe in the Arms of God* (Nashville, TN: Thomas Nelson Publishers, 2003), 81.
2. "Downstairs at the White House: Green Room," *Mr. Lincoln's White House*, https://mrlincolns whitehouse.org/the-white-house/downstairs-at-the-white-house/downstairs-white-house-green-room/.

WHAT'S UP WITH HEAVEN?

2 PETER 3:10–18

*In this lesson we learn about the future that is
ahead of us one day in heaven.*

Everything that is most precious to you and me, everything that is important to Christ followers, is currently in heaven. Once we pass through its magnificent gates, either by death or by being caught up with Christ at the Rapture—heaven will be our home. Learn more about the place where we will spend eternity.

OUTLINE

I. The Place We Soon Shall See

    A. Our Real Estate Is in Heaven

    B. Our Redeemer Is in Heaven

    C. Our Relationships Are in Heaven

    D. Our Residence Is in Heaven

    E. Our Riches Are in Heaven

II. **The People We Now Should Be**
   A. We Should Be People of Purity
   B. We Should Be People of Promise
   C. We Should Be People of Purpose
   D. We Should Be People of Persistence
   E. We Should Be People of Progress

OVERVIEW

As far as we can determine, there is no city or community called "Heaven" today. But there used to be. According to the Texas State Historical Association, the settlement of Heaven, Texas, was organized in 1924. Other than the name, Heaven's main attraction seems to have been its proximity to the Atchison, Topeka, and Santa Fe Railroad.

Sadly, things didn't pan out for the residents of Heaven. It got caught up in a bitter struggle with its neighbor, Morton, Texas, in 1925. Both wanted to be recognized as the Cochran County seat. There was an election that year, and Morton won. Unsatisfied, Heaven contested the results but to no avail. Soon after, the township of Heaven was abandoned.[1]

It sounds humorous to imagine a group of people trying to set up their version of heaven on earth, but it does bring up the question, what will the real heaven be like?

The Place We Soon Shall See

Once the Rapture occurs or we leave this earth through death, we will see the place we call heaven. Think of the joy that will be ours when we get to heaven and see the One who gave His life for us so that we could spend forever with Him in paradise!

Our Real Estate Is in Heaven
The word *heaven* is mentioned almost seven hundred times in the Bible. The language of the Bible speaks of heaven as a place that is high, lofty,

and lifted up. In the Upper Room on the night before His death, Jesus said, "Let not your heart be troubled; you believe in God, believe also in Me. In My Father's house are many mansions; if it were not so, I would have told you. I go to prepare a place for you . . . . I will come again and receive you to Myself; that where I am, there you may be also" (John 14:1–3).

After telling His disciples that He would die on the Cross, Jesus explained that He would be buried, resurrected, and return to heaven. They were saddened by this thought, but He assured them with these comforting words: "I go to prepare a place for you."

In Ephesians 1:20 the apostle Paul also spoke of Christ ascending to heaven to sit at God's right hand "in the heavenly places."

Heaven is not a blissful state of mind; it is a specific place. Sometimes it is referred to as a country or a celestial city, which calls to mind buildings, streets, residents, and activity. Our Father's house is a real place that He has prepared for us. One day He will welcome us to our eternal home—heaven.

Our Redeemer Is in Heaven

The moment we arrive in heaven, we will see Jesus! "Christ has not entered the holy places made with hands, which are copies of the true, but into heaven itself, now to appear in the presence of God for us" (Hebrews 9:24). Right now we don't see Him with our visual eyesight, but when Jesus returns for us, "we shall be like Him, for we shall see Him as He is" (1 John 3:2). The book of Revelation describes what it will be like: "The throne of God and of the Lamb shall be in it, and His servants shall serve Him. They shall see His face" (Revelation 22:3–4).

Think of the joy that will be ours when we get to heaven and see the face of the One who gave His life for us.

Our Relationships Are in Heaven

I remember a conversation I had with my father toward the end of his life. He was a great man who had developed many relationships, which meant he both attended and presided over more than his share of funerals.

He told me, "You know, David, one of the things about getting old is this: One day you begin to realize you have more friends in heaven than you have here on earth."

He was right about that. But as our loved ones who die in Christ pass on to heaven, we have confidence that one day we will join them. Knowing that we will not only see our Redeemer in heaven one day but also those who went on before us makes heaven even more desirable.

Our Residence Is in Heaven

If you are asked about where you live, you might mention your city or state, but for the believer in Christ, heaven is where our true citizenship lies. This is how pastor Steven Lawson described our true home country: "We will live in a world that is spiritually clean from the pollution of all sin . . . . No abortion clinics, no divorce courts, no brothels, no bankruptcy courts, no psychiatric wards, and no treatment centers . . . . There will be no wars, no financial worries . . . . No heart monitors . . . no false teachers, no financial shortages, no hurricanes, no bad habits . . . . We will never need to confess sin. Never need to apologize again . . . . Never have to resist temptation."[2]

We are not citizens of earth going to heaven; we are citizens of heaven traveling through earth. Heaven is our ultimate residence.

Our Riches Are in Heaven

For the believer, heaven is where our riches are stored. "Do not lay up for yourselves treasures on earth, where moth and rust destroy and where thieves break in and steal; but lay up for yourselves treasures in heaven, where neither moth nor rust destroys and where thieves do not break in and steal. For where your treasure is, there your heart will be also" (Matthew 6:19–21).

What a tremendous thought—our treasures are in heaven—through the investments we have made in God's work. We can't take our money with us to heaven, nor our homes, cars, or anything else that is tangible. But we can take other people with us by investing our lives and resources in sharing God's Kingdom. So if you are trying to build equity in heaven, invest your time, talents, and treasure in the Word of God and the souls of men and women who need the message of Jesus Christ.

The People We Now Should Be

How we view the future has a tremendous influence on how we conduct ourselves in the present. The Bible tells us to "set your mind on things above, not on things on the earth" (Colossians 3:2). And Peter offered five characteristics that we should display as we await the Rapture.

We Should Be People of Purity

First, the apostle Peter described the lifestyle of a Christ-follower. "Therefore, since all these things will be dissolved, what manner of persons ought you to be in holy conduct and godliness" (2 Peter 3:11). He said we ought to be people who display holy conduct. The apostle John agreed, "All who have this hope in him purify themselves, just as he is pure" (1 John 3:3 NIV).

We Should Be People of Promise

In addition to pursuing godliness and holy conduct, Peter encouraged Christ-followers to be "looking for and hastening the coming of the day of God" (2 Peter 3:12). In other words, Peter instructed us to be mindful of God's promises for the future, specifically the Rapture and the Second Coming. According to Peter, it is easy to become indifferent to the coming of the Lord and His future plans for us. When Peter wrote that we are "hastening" the coming of the day of God, he was reminding us to earnestly desire the coming of the Lord. Paul said it this way, "Finally, there is laid up for me the crown of righteousness, which the Lord, the righteous Judge, will give to me on that Day, and not to me only but also to all who have loved His appearing" (2 Timothy 4:8).

We are to live in anticipation of that day because we have His sure promise of His return.

We Should Be People of Purpose

Because the Rapture and heaven are a future reality, Peter urged believers in Jesus to remain mindful about their purpose. He wrote, "Therefore, beloved, looking forward to these things, be diligent to be found by Him in peace, without spot and blameless" (2 Peter 3:14).

The instruction to "be diligent" means "to do your best, make haste, take care." Because Christ is coming back, we're to be filled with urgency. Jesus affirmed this instruction when He told us, "Do business till I come" (Luke 19:13). The Lord has assigned work for us to do, and we should serve the Lord with zeal each day as we await His return.

We Should Be People of Persistence

In 2 Peter 3:17, we read, "You therefore, beloved, since you know this beforehand, beware lest you also fall from your own steadfastness, being led away with the error of the wicked." The word "beware" is the translation of a Greek military term that means "to guard or to be on guard." Because Christ is returning soon, we are to constantly guard against being deceived by the error of unbelievers, and because of that deception, lose our own steadfastness.

The word "steadfast" means "to be firmly fixed, constant, unchanging, steady." That term is associated throughout the New Testament with the coming of the Lord and His plan for the future. Because this is no time for weakness, the Bible says, "But hold fast what you have till I come" (Revelation 2:25). And He reminds us, "Behold, I am coming quickly! Hold fast what you have, that no one may take your crown" (Revelation 3:11).

Because we know the truth about the future, we walk patiently in this world, unfazed by the errors of the wicked around us. They may mock us, oppose us, and try to intimidate us, but we are to hold our heads high with our eyes on heaven's future. Be steadfast people!

We Should Be People of Progress

The last recorded words of Peter are: "But grow in the grace and knowledge of our Lord and Savior Jesus Christ. To Him be the glory both now and forever. Amen" (2 Peter 3:18). He is giving us a challenge to occupy our attention until we enter heaven. We are to keep growing in "the grace and knowledge of our Lord." How do we do that? The Bible offers four ways to do that.

First, growth comes through the will of God. It is His desire for us to grow in all areas of life, and God has given us the ability to accomplish that goal. Paul wrote, "Being confident of this very thing, that He who has begun a good work in you will complete it until the day of Jesus Christ" (Philippians 1:6).

Second, growth comes through the watchfulness of prayer. Peter wrote, "But the end of all things is at hand; therefore be serious and watchful in your prayers" (1 Peter 4:7). All Christians understand that prayer is an important component in our walk with God, but the question is: Do we pray as we should? If not, we won't be people of progress.

Third, growth comes through the Word of God. Jesus told us, "Behold, I am coming quickly! Blessed is he who keeps the words of the prophecy of this book" (Revelation 22:7). A. W. Tozer said it this way, "Nothing less than a whole Bible can make a whole Christian."[3]

Finally, growth comes through the work of the Church. Believers are to be a part of a community, a kingdom, a church. The author of Hebrews wrote, "Let us consider one another in order to stir up love and good works, not forsaking the assembling of ourselves together, as is the manner of some, but exhorting one another, and so much the more as you see the Day approaching" (Hebrews 10:24–25).

The coming of Christ and the doctrine of eternity provide the strongest motivations for living the Christian life. The Rapture makes us mindful of heaven even now, moving us onward toward purity, promise, purpose, persistence, and progress.

In heaven, there is a registry called the Lamb's Book of Life, in which the names of all who will be in heaven are recorded. Jesus gave this counsel to His disciples: "Nevertheless do not rejoice in this, that the spirits are subject to you, but rather rejoice because your names are written in heaven" (Luke 10:20). One day you'll stand before God, and He will say to you, "Why should I let you into My heaven?"

You must be able to say, "My name is in the Lamb's Book of Life. I have put my trust in Jesus Christ as my Savior, and, therefore, I qualify to come in through His shed blood." That is your assurance of being in heaven one day.

APPLICATION

Personal Questions

1. What does it mean that our real estate is in heaven?

2. Read Revelation 22:3–4. What emotion do you think will be foremost in your mind in that moment when you see your Redeemer?

3. Read Luke 19:11–13. List two ways that you want to be diligent to "do business till" He comes.

4. Knowing our loved ones are in heaven gives us hope for not only a reunion with them but with our Savior. If you have loved ones or friends who do not know the Lord, how does the knowledge that they won't be in heaven spur you on to witness to them?

5. Recognizing that your citizenship is in heaven, list three things that are of lesser importance to you now.

6. List three things that you want to purpose in your heart to do while you await Christ's return.

7. Read Matthew 6:19–21. How can you lay up for yourself riches in heaven?

8. According to this lesson, what are the four ways that we can experience growth in our walk with God?

Group Questions

1. Discuss as a group what it means to have our real estate and our riches in heaven.

2. Read 2 Peter 3:10–18 together. Discuss the five characteristics we should display as people who are ready for the Rapture.

3. Read Luke 19:13 as a group. Share with each other ways that you want to be diligent to "do business till" He comes.

4. Discuss the four ways mentioned in this lesson that can help us experience growth in our walk with God.

5. Read 1 John 3:3. As a group, talk about practical ways to employ this verse in your personal lives.

6. Read Hebrews 10:24–25. Share ways that you can put this verse into action in your small group, in your family, and in your personal life.

DID YOU KNOW?

The attractions of heaven are too many to enumerate, but there is one benefit that outweighs them all. Max Lucado said it this way, "We may speak about a place where there are no tears, no death, no fear, no night; but those are just the benefits of heaven. The beauty of heaven is seeing God."[4] Being in the presence of our loving Creator, our gracious Redeemer, and our everlasting Father for all eternity will be bliss beyond compare—it will truly make heaven, heaven.

Notes
1. Charles G. Davis, "Heaven, Texas," *Texas State Historical Association*, January 1, 1995, https://www.tshaonline.org/handbook/entries/heaven-tx.
2. Randy Alcorn, *Eternal Perspectives: A Collection of Quotations on Heaven, the New Earth, and Life After Death* (Carol Stream, IL: Tyndale House Publishers, 2012), 377.
3. A. W. Tozer, *Of God and Men: Cultivating the Divine/Human Relationship* (Chicago, IL: Moody Press, 2015), 67.
4. Max Lucado, *When God Whispers Your Name* (Nashville, TN: Thomas Nelson, 1999), 173.

LESSON 6

WHY THE DELAY?

2 PETER 3:8-9

*In this lesson we discover the reasons why we are
still waiting for the Lord to return.*

Nearly two thousand years after Jesus said He would return, we are
still waiting. So you may be tempted to ask, why the delay? Why
hasn't our Savior come back for us? It's frustrating to wait. It tries our
patience and our confidence. But God has not forgotten His promises, and
He has His reasons for delaying His return—and some of them may surprise you. In fact, you might be one of those reasons.

OUTLINE

I. **The Lord's Perspective**

II. **The Lord's Patience**

III. **The Lord's Preference**

OVERVIEW

If you've ever traveled by airplane, flight delays have probably challenged your patience. When airlines give us a timetable, we build our plans around it and expect them to stay on schedule. But when tempted to fly off the handle, simply remember to be thankful you weren't aboard United Airlines flight 857 from San Francisco to Shanghai in March of 2012.

The plane departed San Francisco at 2 p.m. on a Sunday afternoon. Total flight time was scheduled at thirteen hours. Three hours in, however, the plane was diverted to Anchorage, Alaska. The problem had to do with the bathrooms. There weren't enough functional lavatories to ensure everyone's comfort on such a long flight.

When the plane landed in Anchorage, passengers were forced to remain on board for ninety minutes while air-traffic controllers arranged a gate. The travelers were given vouchers for a single meal and a hotel, then told to return the next day to resume their journey to Shanghai.

Another day, another delay. The new flight was scheduled to depart at 1 p.m. on a replacement plane, but the vehicle just sat there for more than two hours. Then, after boarding, passengers were informed the replacement plane was also malfunctioning. They pried themselves out of their seats, retrieved their luggage, and returned to the terminal once again. On Tuesday, a third plane finally departed Anchorage and successfully delivered its passengers to Shanghai—three days late, but thankfully safe and sound.[1]

People don't like delays in general, but it's especially frustrating when we don't understand why we're being forced to wait. That's true of waiting during a trip, at a doctor's office, in the grocery line, in traffic, or for a package to arrive.

It's also true of waiting for God to deliver His promises—including His promise of the Rapture. After all, the very first verse of the book of Revelation says: "The Revelation of Jesus Christ, which God gave Him to show His servants—things which must shortly take place" (1:1). Notice the word—"shortly." If someone says, "I'm going to go down to the store for a gallon of milk, but I'll be back shortly," you wouldn't expect them to be gone for two days, let alone two thousand years!

The final chapter of Revelation uses the word "quickly" to describe the return of Christ that will initiate the End Times. In fact, you can find the word "quickly" used four times in Revelation 22. In verse 12, Jesus said, "Behold, I am coming quickly." And in verse 20 He repeated His promise, saying, "Surely I am coming quickly." For centuries, believers have echoed John's response to that promise: "Amen. Even so, come, Lord Jesus!" (verse 20).

Yet our Lord Jesus has not yet returned. For two thousand years, Christians have watched and waited for the catalyst of the Rapture to coalesce into the next phase in God's prophetic plan. And we are still waiting. It's fair to ask the question: Why the delay?

The Lord's Perspective

Would you believe people were asking that same question in the first century? When the apostle Peter wrote his second epistle to the churches in Asia Minor (modern-day Turkey), he likely did so from the depths of a prison in Rome. Condemned to die by Emperor Nero, Peter's goal for that letter was to confront false teachers who had permeated the Church and to correct the doctrinal confusion they had caused.

Interestingly, one of the questions people in the Early Church seemed to be asking is the same one that puzzles us today: Why the delay?

By that time it had been almost forty years since Jesus died, rose again, and ascended into heaven with the promise to "prepare a place" for His followers (John 14:3). The Early Church was aware of that promise, and many wondered why it was taking so long.

In fact, as Peter noted, false teachers were already using the delay to cast doubt on God's faithfulness and the dependability of Christ's promised return. "Scoffers will come in the last days, walking according to their own lusts, and saying, 'Where is the promise of His coming? For since the fathers fell asleep, all things continue as they were from the beginning of creation' " (2 Peter 3:3–4).

The biblical phrase "last days" refers to the period of time between the end of Jesus' public ministry and the moment of the Rapture. The Christians of Peter's generation were part of the "last days," just as we are. In their time, as in ours, false teachers attempted to cast doubt upon the reality of Christ's return by pointing out that Christ had not yet returned as He had promised.

So how did Peter respond? First, by reminding his readers that our human perspective on time is different from God's perspective. He told them: "But, beloved, do not forget this one thing, that with the Lord one day is as a thousand years, and a thousand years as one day" (2 Peter 3:8). That verse contains an allusion to Psalm 90:4, which states: "A thousand years in Your sight are like yesterday when it is past, and like a watch in the night." The psalmist's point (and Peter's as well) is simple and logical. Because God is eternal, He experiences time differently than we do.

The Bible is God's Book, and the words represent His vocabulary. We have to understand how He is using the words, how He intends for us to understand them, and what He means by them from His perspective. We have to study the Scripture in context.

New Testament scholar Douglas Moo explains:

God views the passing of time from a different perspective than we do. We are impatient, getting disturbed and upset by even a short delay; God is patient, willing to let centuries and even millennia go by as He works out His purposes. Peter is not telling his readers that they are wrong to believe that Christ's return is "imminent." What he is telling them is that they are wrong to be impatient when it does not come as quickly as they might like or hope.[2]

The Bible teaches that God exists in the past, present, and future at the same moment. For God, later is the same as earlier. The end is the same as the beginning. Now is the same as then.

This is a great mystery, and it's hard for us to wrap our heads around the concept of an eternal God. But if God were anything less than eternal, He would not, in actuality, be God. From the perspective of eternity, the Lord Jesus has only been gone for two days! If one day with the Lord is like one thousand years, and if and one thousand years is like one day, then from God's perspective, Jesus hasn't been gone for as long as it seems to us.

"Loved ones," Peter said, in essence, "don't forget this one thing. This is important—this is significant. Remember that God doesn't work on our timetable. His plans are based on His perspective and His perception, not ours."

The Lord's Patience

The second reason for the Lord's delay in returning to this earth is found in verse 9. "The Lord is not slack concerning His promise, as some count slackness, but is longsuffering toward us."

Some of the false teachers in the Early Church were claiming God is slow to carry out His promise—that He is unconcerned, that He doesn't care. But Peter said it's better to take God's delay in the other direction. This delay in the coming of Christ is not because of lack of concern but is actually a sign of how much He cares for and loves people. He's waiting because He's patient. He wants people to come to Him before it is too late.

In the book of Joel, we read, "Rend your heart, and not your garments; return to the Lord your God, for He is gracious and merciful, slow to anger, and of great kindness; and He relents from doing harm" (Joel 2:13). And Paul asked, "Do you despise the riches of His goodness, forbearance, and longsuffering, not knowing that the goodness of God leads you to repentance?" (Romans 2:4).

John Piper wrote, "Since our God is immortal, does not age, does not forget, sees all history at a glance and is never bored, He clearly does not experience time like we do. . . . Don't fail to recognize this. It is no argument against Christ's second coming that almost 2,000 years have passed since His departure. From God's experience of time it is as though Christ just arrived at His right hand the day before yesterday."[3]

Another author said it like this: "Instead of casting doubt on his promise, God's seeming delay actually highlights his heart! His waiting isn't due to his impotence but to his mercy."[4]

The importance of this should not be lost on us. If Jesus had come in the year 500, or in the year 1500, or if He had come in, say, 1875, none of us would have yet been born. You would not have been able to enjoy your daily walk with Jesus Christ. You would not have been able to relish the promises in the Word of God. You would not have been able to look forward to eternal life. Had Jesus come in an earlier era none of us would have been around, none of us would have been caught up in the Rapture, and none of us would have been resurrected. But because of His patience, the epochs of time have been extended to include even us in His redemptive and glorious grace. Thank You, Jesus, for Your patience!

The Lord's Preference

Finally, we come to God's desire regarding the timing of the Rapture. Jesus has delayed His coming because He is "not willing that any should perish but that all should come to repentance" (2 Peter 3:9). That is God's preference.

In the book of Ezekiel, the Lord says, "Do I have any pleasure at all that the wicked should die? . . . And not that he should turn from his ways and live?" (18:23).

God longs for people to come to repentance. He wants to give people every opportunity to change their minds and return to Him and to His ways. "True Christian repentance involves a heartfelt conviction of sin, a contrition over the offense to God, a turning away from the sinful way of life, and a turning towards a God-honoring way of life."[5]

Remember the story of the Prodigal Son. Even though the son had wounded and abandoned his dad with disdain and disrespect, the father waited patiently for his wayward son to come back to him, loving him the whole time he was waiting, looking for him from the front porch, longing for him to come home.

That is God's preference for all people today—that we would end our rebellion and come back to Him.

Speaking of coming back, have you heard of the wonderful partnership between Greyhound bus lines and the National Runaway Safeline—an organization that serves and supports youths who have run away from home? Because of this partnership, any child between the ages of 12 and 21 who has run away from their parents or guardians can receive a free ticket home.

Better still, the organizations provide more than transportation. They partner with the parents and the youth to create a plan for returning home safely—and for working through the issues that led the child to run away in the first place. The family is connected with people and resources in their community that provide long-term support.[6]

It's not possible for any person to physically run away from God. Our Heavenly Father is present in every place and knows everything that can be known. But it is possible to turn away from God's goodness and love. To rebel against His authority. Even to reject Him and remove ourselves from the protection of His lovingkindness.

If that's the case for you, why not return today? There's no ticket necessary. No distance to travel or red tape to cut through. Just turn back. God is always waiting to welcome you with open arms.

APPLICATION

Personal Questions

1. Has there ever been a time in your life when you were frustrated by a delay? What happened? What was the reason for the delay?

2. What was happening in the Early Church because Christ hadn't yet returned?

3. Read 2 Peter 3:8–9.

    a. What does Peter urge you to remember when you are tempted to doubt that the Lord will return?

    b. How is God's relationship to time different from yours?

    c. According to verse 9, what does God's delay prove about His character?

    d. How have you experienced God's patience in fulfilling His promises?

4. Read Joel 2:13.

    a. What five attributes of God does Joel highlight in this verse?

    b. How are we to respond to these attributes?

5. According to Romans 2:4, what leads a person to repentance?

6. What is true Christian repentance?

7. Whom can you tell about God's patience and His desire for people to turn to Him?

Group Questions

1. Share with the group about a time in your life when you were frustrated by a delay. What happened? What was the reason for the delay?

2. Read 2 Peter 3:8 together.

   a. What does Peter urge Christians to remember when they are tempted to doubt that the Lord will return?

   b. How is God's relationship to time different from ours?

3. According to 2 Peter 3:9, what does God's delay prove about His character? What does it *not* prove?

4. Read Joel 2:13 as a group. Discuss the five attributes of God that Joel highlights in this verse and our response to them.

5. According to Romans 2:4, what leads a person to repentance?

6. Discuss what true Christian repentance is.

7. Discuss how Christians can respond to those who scoff at the promise that Jesus will return to this world.

DID YOU KNOW?

The Greek verb for "longsuffering" that Peter used in 2 Peter 3:9 is *makrothumeo*, a combination of two words: long and passion. The combination of the words carries the idea of being under stress for a long period of time—thus the idea of suffering long or being patient. In the New Testament, *makrothumeo* is most often used when referring to patience with people, not circumstances. Longsuffering is listed as one aspect of the fruit of the Spirit in Galatians 5:22. When a person becomes a Christian, God's Spirit gives them the ability not to give way to anger and resentment, to suffer through those times without reacting negatively, and to endure wrongs, criticism, irritations, and unpleasantness. After all, if God has been so patient with us, how can we not be patient with others?

Notes
1. Mike M. Ahlers and Lizzie O'Leary, "Broken Toilets Strand United Passengers in Alaska," *CNN*, March 21, 2012, https://www.cnn.com/2012/03/21/travel/alaska-passengers-stranded/index.html.
2. Douglas J. Moo, *The NIV Application Commentary 2 Peter, Jude* (Grand Rapids, MI: Zondervan, 1996), 260.
3. John Piper, quoted by Chris Mueller, "Why Is Christ Taking So Long to Return?" *Media Library*, https://media.faith-bible.net/scripture/2-peter/why-is-christ-taking-so-long-to-return.
4. James Shaddix, *Exalting Jesus in 2 Peter, Jude* (Nashville, TN: B&H Publishing Group, 2018), 121.
5. Sam Storms, "The Christian and Repentance," *The Gospel Coalition*, https://www.thegospel coalition.org/essay/the-christian-and-repentance/.
6. Elizabeth Wolfe and Saeed Ahmed, "Greyhound Is Giving Free Tickets to Runaways Who Want to Return Home," *CNN*, December 31, 2019, https://www.cnn.com/2019/12/31/us/greyhound-runaway-kids-home-free-ticket-trnd/index.html.

SALVATION IN THE TRIBULATION

REVELATION 7 AND 14

In this lesson we learn about salvation during the Tribulation.

Following the Rapture of the Church, the Tribulation will commence, bringing seven years of terror for all who are living on the earth. This time of intense hardship and misery will result in the purification of Israel, the punishment of sinners, and the final opportunity for the lost to hear the Gospel and come to Christ before they die.

OUTLINE

I. **The Picture of the Tribulation**
  A. Seven Years of Surprise
  B. Seven Years of Severity

II. **The Purpose of the Tribulation**
  A. To Purify Israel
  B. To Punish Sinners
  C. To Preach the Gospel

III. The Preaching During the Tribulation
   A. The Preaching of the 144,000
   B. The Prophesying of the Two Witnesses
   C. The Proclamation of the Angel
   D. The Presence of Bibles and Biblical Materials

OVERVIEW

For more than a month, Nadezhda Sukhorukova endured the fury of the Russian army. So did three hundred thousand other residents in the southeast region of Ukraine. Rockets. Tanks. Drones. Artillery fire. Infantry with guns and grenades. The entire city was trapped in a literal war zone with no access to water, no access to electricity, and no communication with the outside world.

When Nadezhda finally managed to escape, she began posting on Facebook so she could inform the rest of the world about the horrors she'd seen, felt, and lived. "The dead lie in the entrances, on the balconies, in the yards," she wrote. "The biggest fear is night shelling. Do you know what night shelling looks like? Like death."

She ended her report with this expression: "My city is dying a painful death."[1]

When I read about the Tribulation, it sounds like what is currently happening in Ukraine—only ten times worse.

The Picture of the Tribulation

According to God's Word, the Tribulation will be a period filled with unprecedented horror, upheaval, persecution, natural disasters, massive slaughter, and political turmoil in the years prior to Christ's Second Coming.

Once the Rapture occurs, the Tribulation will begin. The word *tribulation* is translated from the Greek *thlipsis* and describes the process when grain is crushed. It evokes crushing and pulverizing—grinding a substance into powder. It is a powerful picture of what will happen on earth during the seven years of the Tribulation.

Seven Years of Surprise

Paul's readers were probably asking, "When is this going to happen?" He anticipates the question in 1 Thessalonians 5:1-2: "But concerning the times and the seasons, brethren, you have no need that I should write to you. For you yourselves know perfectly that the day of the Lord so comes as a thief in the night."

Simply put, he is stating that the Rapture will happen suddenly and without warning. Like a thief in the night—it will be unexpected—but once it occurs, the Tribulation will begin.

Seven Years of Severity

Nowhere in Scripture will you find one word or description that says anything good about the Tribulation period (unless it is the promise that it will end after seven years).

Jesus told us that the Tribulation will be a time of terror and horror without precedent. "For then there will be great tribulation, such as has not been since the beginning of the world until this time, no, nor ever shall be. And unless those days were shortened, no flesh would be saved; but for the elect's sake those days will be shortened" (Matthew 24:21-22).

The central chapters in the book of Revelation give us a vivid description of the horrors of the Tribulation. Wars will increase, peace will end, rampant slaughter will occur on the earth, hail and fire will burn up the planet's grass and destroy a third of all the trees, and intense famine will dry up food supplies. Rivers and seas will become too polluted to sustain life. Many rivers will dry up completely. The sun will scorch the earth and its inhabitants like fire. A quarter of the world's population will die from war, starvation, and beastly predators. Giant earthquakes, accompanied by thunder and lightning, will destroy cities. Mountains will crash into the sea, killing a third of the fish. Tidal waves from the cataclysm will sink a third of the world's ships. A massive meteor shower will strike the earth. Ashes and smoke will rise from the devastation and hide the sun and moon from view. Swarms of demonic insects will darken the sun and inflict painful stings. Rampant, epidemic plagues will kill one-third of all mankind. And everyone, from national leaders to servants and slaves, will flee from the cities to hide in caves and under the rocks (see Revelation 6:2-17; 8:8-13; 9:1-20; 16:1-21).

It is not an overstatement to say that the Tribulation period will be hell on earth.

The Purpose of the Tribulation

In our humanity, we wonder why the Tribulation is necessary. But God will not be absent during this time—the Tribulation is planned to accomplish three important goals.

To Purify Israel

The Jewish nation exists as a fulfillment of God's promise to Abraham that He would bless Abraham with a lineage greater than the sand of the sea and the stars of the sky (see Genesis 12:1–3; 15:5). The Jewish nation that is blessed by God has tested God's patience from its very beginning by turning away from Him. But despite her rebellion, God loves Israel and will keep His promise.

The first function of the Tribulation, according to the Bible, is to purge out the rebels among the Jewish people and produce the final conversion of the nation of Israel.

The apostle Paul left no ambiguity as to whether this purging would be effective. He wrote: "And so all Israel will be saved, as it is written: 'The Deliverer will come out of Zion, and He will turn away ungodliness from Jacob; for this is My covenant with them, when I take away their sins'" (Romans 11:26–27).

One day God is going to bring Israel back to Himself, and to do that He will have to deal with the rebellion in the nation.

To Punish Sinners

When you watch what's happening today and see the cruelty to one another, you may wonder, why doesn't God do something? One of these days God's going to bring about righteous punishment on people who have willfully rejected the sovereignty of God in their life. Romans 1:18 says, "The wrath of God is revealed from heaven against all ungodliness and unrighteousness of men."

One who is infinitely good, as God is, rightly abhors evil because evil is the enemy of goodness. Evil is, in fact, like a parasite; it feeds on and destroys good. Therefore, God rightly directs His wrath at evil.

The prophet Nahum explained the nature of God's wrath saying, "The LORD avenges and is furious. The LORD will take vengeance on His adversaries, and He reserves wrath for His enemies; the Lord is slow to anger and great in power, and will not at all acquit the wicked" (Nahum 1:2-3).

One day those who have been perpetuating evil will be held accountable by God. Because He's a good God, He cannot do otherwise. He must be just. He must be righteous.

To Preach the Gospel

The third thing about the Tribulation that catches everybody by surprise is this—it will be a tremendous opportunity to preach the Gospel. Scripture does not require a revival before the Rapture occurs, but after it happens, the greatest revival in the history of the world is going to take place on earth.

The Preaching During the Tribulation

There will be at least four streams of Gospel truth that will be preached during the Tribulation. Even during this time of punishment, God will invite people to come to Himself before it is too late, yielding a great harvest of souls.

The Preaching of the 144,000

On the frontline of God's effort to bring people to Himself during the Tribulation, there will be 144,000 specially chosen Jewish evangelists who will spread out over this earth with the message of salvation. "Then I saw another angel ascending from the east, having the seal of the living God. And he cried with a loud voice to the four angels to whom it was granted to harm the earth and the sea, saying, 'Do not harm the earth, the sea, or the trees till we have sealed the servants of our God on their foreheads.' And I heard the number of those who were sealed. One hundred and forty-four thousand of all the tribes of the children of Israel were sealed" (Revelation 7:2-4).

God will ordain 144,000 Jews for a very special mission during the Tribulation. "After these things I looked, and behold, a great multitude which no one could number, of all nations, tribes, peoples, and tongues, standing before the throne and before the Lamb, clothed with white robes, with palm branches in their hands" (Revelation 7:9). The number of souls that will be saved is so great "no one could number."

The Prophesying of the Two Witnesses
Along with the preaching of the 144,000, God is going to send two witnesses back to earth. As you carefully read the Scripture, you will discover these witnesses are Moses and Elijah. Revelation 11:3 says, "I will give power to my two witnesses, and they will prophesy one thousand two hundred and sixty days, clothed in sackcloth."

They will return to earth and have a dynamic ministry. They will confront human wickedness and discuss the horrid godlessness of worshiping the devil. They will not be loved for their testimony.

Halfway through the Tribulation, the two witnesses will be killed, and according to the Scripture, their bodies will be displayed in the streets of Jerusalem. The world will see these two witnesses lying in state. Suddenly a voice from heaven will be heard saying, "Come up here." A cloud will envelop them, and they will be raptured to heaven as people watch across the world in total astonishment (see Revelation 11:12).

The Proclamation of the Angel
The Bible tells us that God's going to dispatch an angel from heaven who will fly all over the earth proclaiming the message of His saving grace. Revelation 14:6-7 says, "Then I saw another angel flying in the midst of heaven, having the everlasting gospel to preach to those who dwell on the earth—to every nation, tribe, tongue, and people—saying with a loud voice, 'Fear God and give glory to Him, for the hour of His judgment has come; and worship Him who made heaven and earth, the sea and springs of water.'"

The Presence of Bibles and Biblical Materials
When we are gone, there will still be Bibles, devotional books, films, broadcasts, web pages, and Christian literature available. Henry Morris explained: "Millions upon millions of copies of the Bible and Bible portions have been published in all major languages, and distributed throughout the world. . . . Removal of believers from the world at the rapture will not remove the

Scriptures, and multitudes will no doubt be constrained to read the Bible.... Thus, multitudes will turn to their Creator and Savior in those days, and will be willing to give their testimony for the Word of God and even ... their lives as they seek to persuade the world that the calamities it is suffering are judgments from Lord."[2]

During the Tribulation God is going to bring people to Himself, and heaven will be populated with men and women who have come to Christ during this time.

But following Jesus during the Tribulation will exact an incredibly high price, even death. Revelation 6:9–11 says, "When He opened the fifth seal, I saw under the altar the souls of those who had been slain for the word of God and for the testimony which they held. And they cried with a loud voice, saying, 'How long, O Lord, holy and true, until You judge and avenge our blood on those who dwell on the earth?' Then a white robe was given to each of them; and it was said to them that they should rest a little while longer, until both the number of their fellow servants and their brethren, who would be killed as they were, was completed."

When Jesus returns to the earth at the end of the Tribulation, the bodies of these believers who died during those seven years will be resurrected. They will have new heavenly bodies, and they will merge right into the Millennium to serve with Jesus for a thousand years on this earth.

But there is a time in the Tribulation when you could do something that would keep you from ever becoming a Christian. "If anyone worships the beast and his image and receives his mark on his forehead or on his hand, he himself shall also drink of the wine of the wrath of God, which is poured out full strength into the cup of His indignation. He shall be tormented with fire and brimstone in the presence of the holy angels and in the presence of the Lamb. And the smoke of their torment ascends forever and ever; and they have no rest day or night, who worship the beast and his image, and whoever receives the mark of his name" (Revelation 14:9–11).

If you are in the Tribulation and haven't been saved yet and you take the mark of the Beast, you will go to hell, and there's nothing anybody can do for you.

The Lord tells us when it comes to salvation: "Now is the accepted time ... now is the day of salvation" (2 Corinthians 6:2).

APPLICATION

Personal Questions

1. What event will happen "as a thief in the night" (1 Thessalonians 5:1–2)?

2. According to this lesson, when will the Tribulation begin? How long will it last?

3. Read Matthew 24:21–22. Jesus is giving insights into the terror of the Tribulation. What does He say will be done "for the elect's sake"?

4. Why does Israel need to be purified?

5. Read Romans 1:18 and Nahum 1:2–3. Express in your own words how a God who is rich in mercy will also hold workers of iniquity accountable.

6. What are the four streams of Gospel truth that will be available during the Tribulation?

7. Whom do biblical scholars believe are the two witnesses that come back to life to testify about the truth of the Gospel?

8. Read Revelation 14:6–11. What will happen to individuals who accept the mark of the Beast?

9. Read 2 Corinthians 6:2. What is the message for anyone who has not accepted Christ as Savior?

Group Questions

1. Read 1 Thessalonians 5:1–2 together. Discuss how the imagery used here illustrates the unexpected timing of the Rapture.

2. As a group, discuss when the Tribulation will begin, whether there will be birth pangs beforehand, and the turmoil that will be present during the seven-year judgment on the earth.

3. Read Jesus' words in Matthew 24:21–22. Discuss the many aspects of the Tribulation that will make life here on earth so unbearable during that time. What do these verses say will happen "for the elect's sake"?

4. What are the three reasons for the Tribulation? Discuss the justification for each purpose in the lesson.

5. Read Romans 1:18 and Nahum 1:2–3. As a group, discuss the contrast between God's loving mercy and His wrath toward those who perpetrate evil.

6. List and discuss the four streams of Gospel truth that will be available during the Tribulation.

7. Read Revelation 14:9–11 as a group. Discuss the challenge that people will face during the Tribulation regarding accepting the mark of the Beast.

DID YOU KNOW?

The thought of the Tribulation actually happening one day may seem like the sword of Damocles hanging over one's head if you do not know Christ and expect to be present during that time of trouble. Here is a simple poem with the reminder that "today is the day of salvation."

Every page of the Bible says today.
Every tick of the clock says today.
Every beat of your heart says today.
Every obituary column in the newspaper says today.
And all of creation cries out: "Behold, today is the day of salvation."[3]

Notes
1. Neil MacFarquhar and Andrew E. Kramer, "Russians Pound Ukrainian Cities, as Biden Rallies Anti-Kremlin Alliance" *The New York Times*, March 21, 2022, https://www.nytimes.com/2022/03/21/world/europe/kyiv-mariupol-bombed.html.
2. Henry M. Morris, *The Revelation Record* (Wheaton, IL: Tyndale House Publishers, 1983), 119.
3. Paul W. Powell, *The Night Cometh* (Tyler, TX: Paul W. Powell, 2002), 9.

LESSON 8

AT ANY MOMENT

JOHN 14:1–3;
1 THESSALONIANS 5:4–9

*This lesson discusses the doctrine of imminency
and what it means for the return of Christ.*

I f you are a believer in Jesus Christ, the question of when He will return must be part of your thinking. Some people even think of it daily, asking themselves, "What will I be doing when Christ returns for His Bride?" The question isn't if He will return, but when and if there are any barriers to prevent His coming. The answer to that question is that He can come "at any moment."

OUTLINE

I. **The Passages That Introduce Imminency**

II. **The Pronouns That Insist on Imminency**

III. **The Parables That Illustrate Imminency**

IV. The Principle That Involves Imminency

V. The Practices That Interpret Imminency
- A. Consolation
- B. Expectation
- C. Consecration
- D. Examination

OVERVIEW

The teaching about the Rapture is often referred to as the doctrine of imminency. When something is imminent, it can happen at any moment. There are no barriers that need to be removed or any qualifications that need to be met before it occurs. An event that is imminent is not necessarily immediate, but it is an event that could come at any time.

The Rapture of the Church is an imminent event. That means there are no remaining signs yet to be fulfilled, no remaining events that need to take place. Jesus Christ could come at any moment. If we understand that, it changes how we view the future and how we live our everyday life.

The Passages That Introduce Imminency

In John we are introduced to the assurance that Christ's return at the Rapture is imminent. John 14:1–3 says, "Let not your heart be troubled; you believe in God, believe also in Me. In My Father's house are many mansions; if it were not so, I would have told you. I go to prepare a place for you. And if I go and prepare a place for you, I will come again and receive you to Myself; that where I am, there you may be also."

There are two action verbs in that passage. First, Jesus says, "I go to prepare a place for you." That has already come to pass. Jesus did not remain on earth but instead ascended to heaven. He's at the right hand of the Father, making intercession for us. But He's also preparing a place for us. He's getting ready to receive us into His home. We have the promise of His presence with the words, "Where I am, there you may be also."

The second promise is still to come: "If I go and prepare a place for you, *I will come again* and receive you to Myself" (emphasis added). That's His promise to return at the Rapture. There are no preconditions to His return. He is preparing a home for you and me, and when it is time, He will return for His Church.

The apostle Paul wrote of the imminence of Christ's return saying, "But you, brethren, are not in darkness, so that this Day should overtake you as a thief. You are all sons of light and sons of the day. We are not of the night nor of darkness. Therefore let us not sleep, as others do, but let us watch and be sober. For those who sleep, sleep at night, and those who get drunk are drunk at night. But let us who are of the day be sober, putting on the breastplate of faith and love, and as a helmet the hope of salvation. For God did not appoint us to wrath, but to obtain salvation through our Lord Jesus Christ" (1 Thessalonians 5:4–9).

Paul refers to the believers in the city of Thessalonica as "brethren" and "sons of light"—they are believers in Christ. Then Paul gives them the warning to "watch and be sober" so that they will be ready for Christ's imminent return.

We have this assurance that God did not appoint us to wrath. We are not headed toward the Tribulation; we're headed toward the Rapture.

The idea of readiness for His return is found throughout the New Testament as seen in the following passages:

- "Lift up your heads, because your redemption draws near" (Luke 21:28).
- "We ourselves groan within ourselves, eagerly waiting for the adoption" (Romans 8:23).
- "Eagerly waiting for the revelation of our Lord Jesus Christ" (1 Corinthians 1:7).
- "We shall all be changed—in a moment, in the twinkling of an eye" (1 Corinthians 15:51–52).
- "We also eagerly wait for the Savior" (Philippians 3:20).
- "Looking for the blessed hope" (Titus 2:13).
- "You see the Day approaching" (Hebrews 10:25).
- "The coming of the Lord is at hand" (James 5:8).
- "The Judge is standing at the door!" (James 5:9).

- "Behold, I am coming quickly!" (Revelation 22:7).
- "Surely I am coming quickly" (Revelation 22:20).

These references confirm that the return of the Lord can happen at any moment. The Bible does not give us specific information on the date of the Lord's return, so don't be misled by people who try to provide a time for this event.

Jesus could come back today. Every day for a believer should be a day of expectation!

The Pronouns That Insist on Imminency

Today we believe that Christ could come back at any time. But did you know that Paul believed that Jesus would come back during his life? Paul wrote: "*We* who are alive and remain until the coming of the Lord . . . . Then *we* who are alive and remain shall be caught up together with them in the clouds to meet the Lord in the air. And thus *we* shall always be with the Lord" (1 Thessalonians 4:15, 17, emphasis added).

He said, "*We* will be caught up; *we* will be raptured; *we* are going to go be with the Lord." He believed that in his lifetime Jesus Christ would come back. He eagerly anticipated that return. The imminence of Christ's return should spur us to live as Paul did—focused on accomplishing God's work for His Kingdom while there is still time.

The Parables That Illustrate Imminency

To illustrate the imminency of His return, Jesus told stories in the form of parables.

The first parable is about an unexpected thief. A house was broken into by a thief because the master was not watching. The point that Jesus makes is this: If the master of the house had known when the thief was coming, he would have watched and prevented the theft from his home. But the master did not know the hour or the day when the theft would occur. Jesus concludes the parable, and then He tells us what it means. He says, "Therefore you also be ready, for the Son of Man is coming at an hour you do not expect" (Matthew 24:44).

The thief came and robbed that house because no one was expecting it to happen. Jesus is saying, "Don't be like that homeowner. Be prepared. I can return at any moment."

His second story, found in Matthew 24:45–51, is about two servants who worked for the same master. One of the servants was faithful, and the other servant was unfaithful. The master left for a time and placed the servants in charge of his property. The Bible tells us that the good servant faithfully served his master and provided food for his master's house. But the unfaithful servant didn't anticipate the master coming back, so he became drunk, even abusing other servants. He was unprepared for the master's return. Upon his return, the master found the faithful servant being faithful, and the unfaithful servant being unfaithful. The Bible says the faithful servant was rewarded, and the unfaithful servant was punished. The master in the parable is like our Master in heaven who is coming at an unexpected time. It could be today or tomorrow, this century or the next, but we are to be waiting and watching and working until He comes.

And then there is a third parable about the wise and the foolish virgins at a Jewish wedding in Matthew 25:1–13. Robert Thomas paraphrased this parable of Jesus about "ten virgins, five of whom were foolish and five wise . . . . When the bridegroom came unexpectedly in the middle of the night, the foolish virgins had no oil for their lamps. By the time they purchased oil, it was too late, and they found themselves locked out of the wedding feast where the wise virgins had been admitted. Neither group knew a fixed period within which the groom would return, but one group was ready, the other was not."[1]

Jesus tells us, "Watch therefore, for you know neither the day nor the hour in which the Son of Man is coming" (Matthew 25:13). While the coming of the Lord is *certain*, the timing of His coming is *uncertain*. Always be ready so that when He comes, you'll be prepared.

What does it mean to be ready? If you do not know Jesus Christ as your personal Savior, you need to accept Him now. If you're not saved when He comes to take us to heaven in the Rapture, you will be left behind. And for those of us who are Christians, if we're involved in behaviors and activities that are not pleasing to the Lord, now is the time to put those things behind us. Make the decision to live fully consecrated to His ways and purposes in expectation of His return.

The Principle That Involves Imminency

There are many who teach and believe that the Church is not going to be raptured before the Tribulation. But the Bible says, "There is therefore now no condemnation to those who are in Christ Jesus" (Romans 8:1). Christians have not been appointed to wrath but to salvation in Jesus Christ our Lord.

The imminency of Christ's return is more than an incidental truth about the Rapture. The doctrine of imminency is a source of great conflict among some theologians. They ask, "Is it really true that Jesus could come back at any time?" They ask this because if Jesus can come back at any time, then the idea that the Church must go through the Tribulation is false. You will not go through the Tribulation if you're a Christian; you're going to heaven to be with the Lord.

The Practices That Interpret Imminency

As we wait for the Rapture, we are not to look for a sign but for the Lord Himself. Here are four words that describe our practical response to the "at any moment" return of the Lord.

Consolation

In 1 Thessalonians 4:18 Paul says, "Therefore comfort one another with these words."

The Thessalonians wondered if they would see their deceased loved ones again. Paul reminds them death is not final and that all who die in Christ will be restored to bodily life and caught up with Christ when He returns. This thought provided comfort to them then and to us today. Your saved loved ones will be resurrected, and you will meet them in the air for all eternity. We do not sorrow as those "who have no hope" (1 Thessalonians 4:13) because we know that this is not final. We are to comfort one another with these words until He returns.

Expectation

The Bible tells us to cultivate an attitude of continual expectation and to live every day in anticipation of Christ's return.

Let the coming of the Lord motivate you to live in anticipation of that Great Day. Keep reading the Bible, be watchful, and ask God to help you understand the urgency of life. Live in daily expectation of His return.

Consecration

The next action is consecration—to commit ourselves fully to Him. In 1 John 3:2–3 we read, "Beloved, now we are children of God; and it has not yet been revealed what we shall be, but we know that when He is revealed, we shall be like Him, for we shall see Him as He is. And everyone who has this hope in Him purifies himself, just as He is pure."

If we believe He's coming back, we need to purpose in our hearts to be faithfully serving Him when He returns and to pursue sanctification by being transformed into the image of Christ. Our goal should be to consecrate each day to His purpose.

Examination

Suppose the Lord chose this very moment to return. Would you be ready? Jesus warned us that He's coming quickly (see Revelation 22:12). When that moment strikes, there will be no time to get ready. You need to stay ready. So the question you must ask is, have I committed myself to Jesus Christ and submitted to Him as my Lord and Savior?

After Jesus told His disciples that He would leave them to prepare a place for them, He added, "And where I go you know, and the way you know" (John 14:4). Immediately Thomas, said, "Lord, we do not know where You are going, and how can we know the way?" (John 14:5). Jesus responded with one of the most important statements in the Bible. He said, "I am the way, the truth, and the life. No one comes to the Father except through Me" (John 14:6). The *only* way to God is through Jesus Christ.

The Rapture challenges us to live with eternity in view—to make each moment count until Christ returns. The coming of the Lord is imminent; be ready to join Him in the air "at any moment."

APPLICATION

Personal Questions

1. How does the doctrine of imminency affect how you live your life today?

2. Is the idea of being "caught up" in the Rapture something that brings joy and anticipation or fear and concern to you?

3. Write your own definitions of *imminent* and *immediate*.

   a. Imminent:

   b. Immediate:

4. List three ways the Rapture challenges you to live with eternity in view.

5. Read Matthew 24:44–51. What is the Lord saying to the people listening to Him that day and to us as well?

6. Write what the following words mean to you as a follower of Christ waiting for His return.

   a. Consolation:

   b. Expectation:

   c. Consecration:

   d. Examination:

7. Does living in a place where there is persecution affect one's expectation for Christ's return?

8. Why is it important not to neglect Christian fellowship during the days we are living in?

9. If someone asks, "Can I be assured of being in heaven one day?" how would you respond? Write down the verses you would include in your response to that question.

10. Write John 14:6 below and then paraphrase what it means to you.

11. If you thought this would be your last day on earth and that Christ might return, what would you do in expectation of His return?

Group Questions

1. Discuss what the doctrine of imminency means. Does it change how you think about the Rapture? If so, in what way?

2. As a group, discuss the difference between *imminent* and *immediate* regarding Christ's return.

3. Understanding the Rapture is imminent should instill a desire in every Christian to be ready for that day. Discuss what changes this awareness should bring into individual lives.

4. Discuss the parable about the property owner who could have prevented being robbed if he had known when the thief would come, and then relate the applicable truths this story reveals to you. If comfortable, discuss areas of your life where you live as though Jesus' return is not imminent.

5. If you thought this would be your last day on earth, what would you do in expectation of His return? Share your answer with the group.

6. Discuss why it is important not to neglect Christian fellowship during the days leading up to Christ's return.

DID YOU KNOW?

The people of Taiwan understand the practical application of imminence in a visceral way. For more than seventy years, Taiwan has been under threat of invasion from the Chinese Communist Party (CCP), and that threat has intensified in recent years. The citizens of Taiwan don't question if China will attack but are prepared for when they do attack. Huoh Shoou-yeh, who is chairman of a defense ministry think tank, said, "Taiwan must be ready for a conflict at any time."[2] That is the kind of readiness we need to maintain as followers of Jesus. We are on the cusp of a heavenly event (invasion), and we must remain ready for that glorious hour.

Notes

1. Robert L. Thomas, "The Rapture and the Biblical Teaching of Imminency," *Evidence for the Rapture: A Biblical Case for Pretribulationism* (Chicago, IL: Moody Press, 2015), 27.
2. RFA Staff, "Taiwan Must Be Ready for a Chinese Invasion 'At Any Time" Experts Say," Radio Free Asia, November 3, 2022, https://www.rfa.org/english/news/southchinasea/taiwan-invasion-readiness.

DELIVERED
BEFORE
DESTRUCTION

LUKE 17:26–37

In this lesson we learn that God rescues His people from the trials of life and the judgment of the Tribulation.

Throughout the Old Testament there are many examples of God exacting judgment on evildoers. And there are just as many stories of Him rescuing His people from that judgment. Noah and his family were rescued from the Flood that killed every living thing on earth. Lot and his family were rescued from the destruction of the wicked cities of Sodom and Gomorrah. Exodus is devoted to telling the story of God rescuing His chosen people from the plagues that befell Egypt. Rahab the prostitute was rescued from Jericho before that city fell to God's judgment because she feared the Lord and aided His spies. Daniel was rescued from the mouths of lions. Shadrach, Meshach, and Abednego were rescued from the fiery furnace. In the same way, God will rescue His Church by taking us away before the Tribulation.

OUTLINE

I. The Rescue of Noah

II. The Rescue of Lot

III. The Rescue of the Godly

OVERVIEW

The American Embassy in Sudan is located in a well-fortified area just a stone's throw from the Blue Nile River on the western side of Khartoum. It's a relatively new complex of buildings, but it sits in a rough and violent city. In April 2023, a team of special operations forces completed the difficult mission of evacuating the embassy. Chaos was descending on the city, and it was time to airlift the American diplomats to safety.

There were about one hundred people at the embassy, and it took less than an hour to get everyone out. The Navy's SEAL Team Six took part in the mission, which was cloaked in secrecy and executed in darkness. The evacuation was "fast and clean," using two MH-47 Chinook helicopters. American officials said the deteriorating situation required the emergency evacuation because a storm of violence was heading toward the embassy gates.[1]

All of us who know Christ are His ambassadors, His representatives in a deteriorating world. Just before the storm of the Tribulation's violence hits the gates of the Church, our great Commander is literally going to airlift us to safety, rescuing us.

We've talked about that rescue often in these pages—it's the Rapture. But what you may be surprised to learn is that God has followed that pattern many times in history. Proverbs 11:8 says, "The righteous is delivered from trouble, and it comes to the wicked instead." Psalm 144 says, "Part your heavens, Lord, and come down. . . . Reach down your hand from on high; deliver me and rescue me from the mighty waters" (verses 5–7 NIV). While that's not a specific picture of the Rapture, I can visualize the Lord's hand reaching down to snatch us up in deliverance just in the nick of time.

The apostle Paul referred to this aspect of Christ's character when he urged us "to wait for His Son from heaven, whom He raised from the dead, even Jesus who delivers us from the wrath to come" (1 Thessalonians 1:10). In this lesson we will see how this worked out for two families in the Old Testament and what it all means for believers today. By studying the ways God acted to rescue His people in the past, we can learn much that will add to our understanding of God's future rescue of His people at the Rapture.

The Rescue of Noah

When speaking about His return in Luke 17, Jesus used two illustrations from the Old Testament—Noah and Lot. He said, "Just as it was in the days of Noah, so also will it be in the days of the Son of Man. People were eating, drinking, marrying and being given in marriage up to the day Noah entered the ark. Then the flood came and destroyed them all. It was the same in the days of Lot. People were eating and drinking, buying and selling, planting and building. But the day Lot left Sodom, fire and sulfur rained down from heaven and destroyed them all. It will be just like this on the day the Son of Man is revealed" (verses 26–30 NIV).

There's an interesting fact about the flood of Noah's day that's often overlooked. In the genealogies of Genesis 5, we see that Enoch was the father of Methuselah, who was the father of Lamech, who was the father of Noah (see Genesis 5:21–29). Methuselah lived longer than anyone else in history—969 years. His father (who was Noah's great-grandfather), Enoch, was a preacher of righteousness. He preached about the return of Christ. "Now Enoch, the seventh from Adam, prophesied . . . saying, 'Behold, the Lord comes with ten thousands of His saints'" (Jude 14). And Enoch was raptured before the Flood.

Bodie Hodge, an engineer and a student of Genesis, noticed something interesting about those two men: "If you match up the ages of the patriarchs, Methuselah died the same year as the Flood. . . . Methuselah was raised by a godly parent (Enoch) who walked with God and pleased God so that God took him away without death. In fact, Methuselah may have actually helped Noah in the construction phase of the Ark. But his death preceded the Flood."[2]

Pause a minute to let that soak in. Enoch was raptured before the Flood; Methuselah died just days before the Flood. God delivered them both from the coming wrath, and together they represent those who will be raptured and resurrected when Jesus comes in the sky for His people. And don't forget about Noah and his family. God also took them above the waters of the Flood and rescued them from the storm of judgment that fell on the earth.

The Rescue of Lot

Our Lord's other example was the family of Lot. In Genesis 19, two angels were sent by God to evacuate Lot and his family from the wicked city of Sodom before literal fires of judgment fell on that place. At dawn on that fateful day, the angels woke Lot and his family and said, "Hurry! Take your wife and your two daughters who are here, or you will be swept away when the city is punished." The angels physically grabbed the hands of Lot's wife and daughters, dragging them from danger, "for the LORD was merciful to them" (verses 15–16 NIV). As soon as this little family was rescued from Sodom, the God of righteousness sent down bolts of fire that consumed the city in judgment.

Dr. W. A. Criswell, who was a constant student of biblical prophecy, said in a sermon on this subject, "Both of those men, Enoch and Lot, are very typical of God's people in this earth now. Enoch—glorious man who walked with God: and was not, for God took him—Enoch was raptured, he was taken out before the judgment of the Flood came. . . . Lot was taken out also before the great judgment day of God came. . . . All of God's people . . . those who have placed their trust in Him, they will be taken out before that awful day comes."[3]

Of course, these weren't isolated incidents. God's rescue of Noah and Lot is in keeping with the way He has worked throughout history. He spared the Hebrews in Egypt from the plagues of wrath that fell over Pharaoh's empire. The final plague—the death of the firstborn—came nowhere near the Jewish people who painted their doorposts with the blood of the Passover lamb. God made for them a way of escape.

Our same God brought Rahab out of Jericho before judgment fell on that city. He brought Daniel out of the lions' den before the mouths of the lions were opened and devoured their prey. And He rescued Shadrach, Meshach, and Abednego from the fiery furnace. Jesus made sure that His disciples were out of the Garden of Gethsemane, terrified but safe, as He Himself was led away toward the Cross. We worship a Savior who saves!

The Rescue of the Godly

Just as the family of Noah and the family of Lot were evacuated before the onslaught of judgment, so it will be with the family of the Lord. Mirroring the words of Jesus, Peter also talked about this in detail when he wrote:

> If [God] did not spare the ancient world when he brought the flood on its ungodly people, but protected Noah, a preacher of righteousness, and seven others; if he condemned the cities of Sodom and Gomorrah by burning them to ashes, and made them an example of what is going to happen to the ungodly; and if he rescued Lot, a righteous man, who was distressed by the depraved conduct of the lawless . . . then the Lord knows how to rescue the godly from trials and to hold the unrighteous for punishment on the day of judgment (2 Peter 2:5–9 NIV).

The Lord knows how to rescue us from judgment. Of course He does! As Paul wrote to Timothy, his son in the faith, "For to this end we both labor and suffer reproach, because we trust in the living God, who is the Savior of all men, especially of those who believe" (1 Timothy 4:10). That's why Paul, having described the Rapture, told the Thessalonians to "comfort one another with these words" (1 Thessalonians 4:18). We are under the power and protection of Jesus, our Savior.

This is all a part of God's grace to us. He promised, "No temptation has overtaken you except such as is common to man; but God is faithful, who will not allow you to be tempted beyond what you are able, but with the temptation will also make the way of escape, that you may be able to bear it" (1 Corinthians 10:13).

Our Lord has designed a way of escape, a rescue, an evacuation for His people at the end of the age of the Gospel of grace. We call it the Rapture. In this way, the Rapture is an extension of God's character. It reveals who He is and what He values. As the psalmist wrote, "He also brought me out into a broad place; He delivered me because He delighted in me" (Psalm 18:19).

The Lord delights in His Church, in His family. He delights in you. Yes, we suffer trouble and tribulation in this world, but God always makes a way of escape for us because He delights in us. His deliverance isn't just reserved for the Rapture. He wants to deliver you right now from your anxiety about the future and from the worries that are crippling your life.

This theme circulates through Psalm 34 like a springtime fragrance: "I sought the LORD, and He heard me, and *delivered* me from all my fears. . . . The angel of the LORD encamps all around those who fear Him, and *delivers* them. . . . The righteous cry out, and the LORD hears, and *delivers* them out of all their troubles. . . . Many are the afflictions of the righteous, but the LORD *delivers* him out of them all" (verses 4, 7, 17, 19, emphasis added).

The same One—the Lord Jesus Christ—who delivers us over and over from the perils of life will deliver His Church at the end of the age, evacuating us and airlifting us to safety before the onslaught of Tribulation justice.

In her book *Beyond the Storm*, Debra B. Morton describes what happened to her family during Hurricane Katrina. She said that her seventy-year-old dad and stepmom had been evacuated before the storm, but went back home afterward, thinking all was now safe. When the nearby levee gave way, the water began rising in the house. "My father and stepmom (who was on dialysis), along with my sister, her husband, and their children, had to escape to the over one-hundred-degree attic for three days to avoid drowning, as the water (seemingly from nowhere) filled their home. There was nowhere to go."

How could they let anyone know they were trapped in the attic? The frightened little family could hear the chopping sound of helicopters above them, but they had no way of contacting their would-be rescuers. According to Debra, one of the family members finally managed to open a small hole in the roof, just big enough to push a broken compact mirror through. "My father told me he felt in his heart when on that third day the rescuers saw that little mirror reflection." He was right. They did, and the family was rescued on the third day. "There was something about that third day," Debra said, "just like the resurrection story."[4]

Now, our Lord will not need for us to knock a hole in the roof and flash a mirror at Him. He knows where we are, every one of us at every moment. He rose on the third day to deliver us into His eternal Kingdom, and He's coming to rescue us before the levee breaks and the flood of judgment washes over the earth. We feel in our hearts that day is near!

APPLICATION

Personal Questions

1. Recall a time in your life when you were rescued from danger. Describe the situation. How were you delivered?

2. What is your favorite "rescue" story in the Bible?

3. In 1 Thessalonians 1:10 what does Paul say that Jesus will deliver us from?

4. List five biblical examples of God saving His people from trouble.

5. Read Psalm 18:17–19.

   a. Why did the Lord deliver the psalmist from his enemy?

   b. How does this encourage you?

6. Read Psalm 34.

   a. How many times is the word "deliver" (or a form of it) used in the psalm?

   b. Write down three things God saves His people from.

7. Where in your life do you need deliverance? Ask God to rescue you from the trouble you are facing.

8. Take a moment to thank God for the ways you have experienced His deliverance.

Group Questions

1. If comfortable, share about a time in your life when you were rescued from danger. Describe the situation and how you were saved.

2. Discuss your favorite "rescue" stories in the Bible and explain why they are so powerful.

3. Discuss five biblical examples of God saving His people from trouble.

4. Read Psalm 18:17–19 together.

    a. From whom was the psalmist delivered?

    b. What did the Lord do for the psalmist and why?

5. Read Psalm 34 as a group.

    a. Discuss the use of the word "deliver" (or a form of it) in the passage.

    b. What does the Lord deliver His people from according to this psalm?

6. Share with one another the ways you have experienced God's rescue.

7. Spend some time as a group praising God for His mighty acts of deliverance.

DID YOU KNOW?

The apostle Paul wrote that all who belong to Christ have been delivered from the domain of darkness to the "kingdom of the Son" (Colossians 1:13). Yet we are still given instructions in the New Testament for defending ourselves from Satan's attacks (see Ephesians 6:10–18). That is the reason Jesus taught His disciples to pray for deliverance "from the evil one" (Matthew 6:13). Even though the battle is decided, the war continues until the end (see Revelation 20:10). As a Christian, you have been eternally delivered from the power of Satan and are daily delivered by God's grace and power.

Notes
1. Based on multiple news reports the week of April 27, 2023.
2. Bodie Hodge, "Methuselah: When Did He Die?" *Answers in Genesis*, July 30, 2010, https://answersingenesis.org/bible-timeline/genealogy/when-did-methuselah-die/.
3. W. A. Criswell, "God's Churches and the Great Tribulation," W. A. Criswell Sermon Library, https://wacriswell.com/sermons/1961/god-s-churches-and-the-great-tribulation/.
4. Debra B. Morton, *Beyond the Storm: How to Thrive in Life's Toughest Seasons* (Nashville, TN: Nelson Books, 2019), 24–25.

KEPT FROM THE HOUR

REVELATION 3:10

In this lesson we learn three reasons why Christians can be certain they will not live through the Tribulation period.

The Scriptures describe the Tribulation as a seven-year period of widespread unrest, war, pestilence, persecution, natural disasters, and political oppression like nothing that has ever been seen or imagined. Reading about all that the world will undergo, you may wonder—will God save His followers from experiencing this time of strife? Or will we have to endure it for a time? In this lesson, we'll dive into a compelling argument that God will spare His children from experiencing the "hour of trial which shall come upon the whole world" (Revelation 3:10).

OUTLINE

I. **The Scope of This Promise**

II. **The Security of This Promise**

III. The Simplicity of This Promise

IV. The Significance of This Promise

OVERVIEW

The Rapture is a biblical promise stating that one day Jesus will drop everything, bring His people to Himself, and make our deepest dreams come true by welcoming us to His Father's house for all eternity.

While the majority of biblical teachers believe in the Rapture itself, there's honest disagreement about when this great event will occur. Some scholars believe the Rapture will take place at the end of the Tribulation, almost simultaneous to the Second Coming of Christ. Those who hold this view are referred to as post-tribulationists. Others teach the Rapture will happen in the middle of the Tribulation, just before the Great Tribulation begins. They are mid-tribulationists. Also, a relatively new view suggests the Rapture will occur after the midpoint of the Tribulation but before God's seven bowls of wrath have been poured out on the earth. This is the pre-wrath view.

It's important to acknowledge the differences in these lines of thought, even though the preponderance of scriptural evidence makes it clear the Rapture of the Church will take place before the Tribulation occurs, sparing us from the awful seven-year period described in Revelation 6–18.

In this lesson, we're going to closely examine one verse of Scripture that indicates a before-the-tribulation Rapture. It's one of the most important verses in the entire New Testament on this subject and worthy of investigation.

Early in the book of Revelation, the Lord Jesus promised the church at Philadelphia: "Because you have kept My command to persevere, I also will keep you from the hour of trial which shall come upon the whole world, to test those who dwell on the earth" (3:10).

Andrew M. Woods wrote, "Commentators of all stripes readily acknowledge that this verse represents the most significant verse in the debate over the timing of the rapture."[1]

The Scope of This Promise

Revelation 3:10 expresses Christ's message to one of the seven churches to whom the book of Revelation is addressed—the church in the ancient city of Philadelphia. Its significance, however, isn't limited to that congregation. This wasn't just a promise having to do with regional persecution. Jesus wasn't telling the church in Philadelphia, "I'm going to keep you from persecution that's going to come into your vicinity." Instead, He said, "I . . . will keep you from the hour of trial which shall come upon the whole world."

Jesus' promise is intended for all churches, everywhere, throughout all history. That's the scope of Revelation 3:10. The messages to the seven churches are applicable to all the churches in the world. This is why we keep reading in Revelation 2 and 3: "He who has an ear, let him hear what the Spirit says to the churches" (2:7, 11, 17, 29; 3:6, 13, 22). "Thus, the promise of being kept from the hour of testing is not limited to the church at Philadelphia," wrote Michael A. Rydelnik, "but was a promise for the universal church as well."[2]

There's an hour of trial ahead, not just for Asia Minor, but for the globe. It will engulf the entire planet and all those "who dwell on the earth" (Revelation 3:10). John later declared that the trials of the Tribulation period will affect "all nations" (Revelation 12:5) and, again, "the whole world" (Revelation 16:14).

The Security of This Promise

Jesus' promise in Revelation 3:10 provides great security for His followers. Why? Because He isn't going to keep us *through* the Tribulation but *from* the Tribulation. Some scholars teach that the Church will go through the flames of persecution. They believe Christ will be with us and keep us safe in the midst of it—that He will be present with us as we endure the Tribulation.

But that's not what the promise says. Jesus said, "I also will keep you from the hour of trial which shall come upon the whole world, to test those who dwell on the earth" (Revelation 3:10). Not *during* the trial or *in* the trial or *through* the trial but *from* the trial. This requires a removal before the trial ever occurs. Dr. Ryrie gave a vivid illustration of this distinction from a teacher's viewpoint.

As a teacher, I frequently give exams. Let's suppose that I announce an exam will occur on such and such a day at the regular class time. Then suppose I say, "I want to make a promise to students whose grade average for the semester so far is A. The promise is: I will keep you from the exam."

Now I could keep my promise to those A students this way: I would tell them to come to the exam, pass out the exam to everyone, and give the A students a sheet containing the answers. They would take the exam and yet in reality be kept from the exam. They would live through the time but not suffer the trial. This is post-tribulationism: protection while enduring.

But if I said to the class, "I am giving an exam next week. I want to make a promise to all the A students. I will keep you from the hour of the exam." They would understand clearly that to be kept from the hour of the test exempts them from being present during that hour. This is pre-tribulationism, and this is the meaning of the promise of Revelation 3:10. And the promise came from the risen Savior who Himself is the deliverer of the wrath to come (1 Thessalonians 1:10).[3]

If Revelation 3:10 only means the Church will be kept safe during the Tribulation, then we have a problem as we read the rest of Revelation. During the Tribulation, especially during the first half of it, multitudes of people will flee to Christ and be saved. But they will not be safe! The ruthless government of the Antichrist will search them out and slaughter them in terrible ways (Revelation 6:9–11; 11:7; 12:11; 13:7, 15; 14:13; 17:6; 18:24).

On the other hand, if believers will be raptured before the Tribulation, then what security we find in Revelation 3:10. Jesus' promise helps us sleep better and live with greater confidence. It enables us to anticipate our Lord's coming for us at any moment now.

The Simplicity of This Promise

This insight from Revelation 3:10 is centered on one simple, little word. In the Greek language, it has just two letters: *ek,* which are translated "from" in Revelation 3:10.

This preposition is found more than eight hundred times in the New Testament, and it's translated "out of" or "from" (or an equivalent phrase) in virtually every instance. Here is some context:

> *Ek* is rendered *out of* hundreds of times, as for example: "*Out of* Egypt have I called My Son" (Matthew 2:15); "first *cast out* the beam *out of* thine own eye" (Matthew 7:5); "for *out of* the heart proceed evil thoughts" (Matthew 15:19); "And [many bodies of the saints] came *out of* the graves after His resurrection" (Matthew 27:53); "I will spew thee *out of* My mouth" (Revelation 3:16).[4]

The promise is clear and plain: "I . . . will keep you *from* the hour of testing." Not just from any persecution but from the coming time that will affect the whole earth.[5]

Sometimes we make studying Scripture way more complicated than it needs to be. God's promise is simple. He will keep us "from" (*ek*) the hour of trial that will come upon the whole world.

The Significance of This Promise

With all that said, however, there is a significant truth we must accept. Just because Christians will be spared from the torment described in Revelation 3:10, we are not exempted from trials and suffering beforehand. Actually, the Bible promises the exact opposite.

Jesus said, "If the world hates you, you know that it hated Me before it hated you" (John 15:18). He added, "In the world you will have tribulation; but be of good cheer, I have overcome the world" (John 16:33). The apostle Paul wrote, "Yes, and all who desire to live godly in Christ Jesus will suffer persecution" (2 Timothy 3:12). And Peter said, "Beloved, do not think it strange concerning the fiery trial which is to try you, as though some strange thing happened to you" (1 Peter 4:12).

Jesus' promise to rapture Christians before the Tribulation is a specific declaration that applies to a specific moment. We will be spared from the reign of the Antichrist. But in the meantime, we will still endure the persecution all of God's saints have endured throughout history.

In his book *Kept From the Hour*, Dr. Gerald B. Stanton helps us understand why Christians suffer now but won't suffer then: "Today, suffering is often the portion of the Christian, but not wrath. Wrath is reserved for unbelievers."[6]

The Tribulation represents the outpouring of God's wrath on the evil of this world. The Bible says, "God did not appoint us to wrath, but to obtain salvation through our Lord Jesus Christ" (1 Thessalonians 5:9). Paul wrote, "Much more then, having now been justified by His blood, we shall be saved from wrath through Him" (Romans 5:9).

As I studied this subject, I underlined these words from Dr. John F. Walvoord: "Paul is expressly saying that our appointment is to be caught up to be with Christ; the appointment of the world is for the Day of the Lord, the day of wrath. One cannot keep both of these appointments."[7]

The unsaved will keep the appointment with the day of wrath—the Tribulation. The saved will keep the appointment with Christ when we are drawn from the earth in the pre-tribulation Rapture.

Have you heard of "The Great Raid"? It took place near the end of World War II in 1945. After General Douglas MacArthur and U.S. forces landed in the Philippines, orders went out from the Japanese military to kill any prisoners of war on the verge of being rescued. Many U.S. soldiers were shot and burned alive within weeks or even days of potential freedom.

A camp called Cabanatuan was one of the largest facilities for prisoners of war—and one of the most notorious. Knowing that the Japanese were likely to kill the POWs if U.S. forces got too close, MacArthur decided to send a secret rescue operation to liberate those prisoners before allowing his armies to advance.

The raid took place on January 30. More than one hundred Army Rangers, Alamo Scouts, and Filipino guerrillas trekked thirty miles behind enemy lines until they located the camp, overwhelmed the guards, and set the prisoners free.

In the end, 513 POWs were rescued on that day from certain death. The rescuing force suffered only two casualties, making The Great Raid one of the most successful rescue missions ever conducted.[8]

The Rapture will likewise be a rescue mission. The just judgment of God's wrath is on the way. It will crash against the sinfulness and unrighteousness of our world like waves smashing through sand. Yet those who call on the Name of the Lord shall be saved—not in the midst of those waves, but from them. We shall be kept safe from the hour of God's wrath.

APPLICATION

Personal Questions

1. When in your life did someone break a promise they made to you? How did that experience make you feel?

2. What are some of your favorite promises in the Bible? Why are they important to you?

3. How would you summarize Revelation 3:10 in your own words?

4. How do we know that the promise in Revelation 3:10 is for all churches, everywhere, throughout all history?

5. What is the difference between being kept from the Tribulation and being kept through the Tribulation?

6. What is the key Greek word that proves the simplicity of God's promise to keep believers out of the Tribulation period? What are the ways it is translated in the Bible?

7. Read John 16:33, 2 Timothy 3:12, and 1 Peter 4:12.

   a. What do these verses say believers can expect *before* the Tribulation?

   b. How can these verses strengthen your faith when you are walking through a trial?

8. How are you experiencing God's help in the midst of your struggles today?

Group Questions

1. As a group, discuss the power of a promise broken and a promise kept.

2. Share your favorite promises in the Bible with the group. Describe why they are so significant.

3. What is the promise of Revelation 3:10?

4. Discuss the difference between being kept *from* the Tribulation and being kept *through* the Tribulation.

5. Discuss the key Greek word that proves the simplicity of God's promise to keep believers out of the Tribulation period and the ways it is translated in the Bible.

6. Read John 16:33, 2 Timothy 3:12, and 1 Peter 4:12 as a group. How do these verses provide strength to you when you are going through a time of trial?

7. If you comfortable in doing so, share with the group how you have experienced God's help in a difficult time. Whom in your life can you encourage with God's promises?

DID YOU KNOW?

The late professor Lewis Smedes wrote this about promises: "What a marvelous thing a promise is! When a person makes a promise, she reaches out into an unpredictable future and makes one thing predictable: she will be there even when being there costs her more than she wants to pay. When a person makes a promise, he stretches himself out into circumstances that no one can control and controls at least one thing: he will be there no matter what the circumstances turn out to be. With one simple word of promise, a person creates an island of certainty in a sea of uncertainty."[9] In our world of uncertainty, Almighty God has given us the promise of Revelation 3:10—that He will not forsake His people.

Notes

1. Andrew M. Woods, "John and the Rapture: Revelation 2–3," in *Evidence for the Rapture: A Biblical Case for Pretribulationism*, ed. John F. Hart (Chicago, IL: Moody Publishers, 2015), 196.
2. Michael A. Rydelnik, "Israel: Why the Church Must Be Raptured Before the Tribulation," in *Evidence for the Rapture: A Biblical Case for Pretribulationism*, ed. John F. Hart (Chicago, IL: Moody Publishers, 2015), 264.
3. Charles Ryrie, Come Quickly, *Lord Jesus: What You Need to Know About the* Rapture (Eugene, OR: Harvest House Publishing, 1996), 130–131.
4. *Our Hope Magazine*, August 1950, 86.
5. Charles Ryrie, *Come Quickly, Lord Jesus: What You Need to Know About the Rapture* (Eugene, OR: Harvest House Publishing, 1996), 137.
6. Gerald B. Stanton, Kept *From the Hour* (Miami Springs, FL: Schoettle Publishing, 1991), 44–45.
7. John F. Walvoord, *The Thessalonian Epistles* (Grand Rapids, MI: Zondervan, 1974), 54.
8. Val Lauder, "Remember 'The Great Raid' of 1945," CNN, January 29, 2015, https://edition.cnn.com/2015/01/29/opinion/lauder-great-raid-cabanatuan-pow-camp-1945/index.html.
9. Lewis Smedes, "Keeping Promises," *Preaching Today*, https://www.preachingtoday.com/illustrations/2001/august/13189.html.

LESSON 11

DEAD SILENCE

SELECTED SCRIPTURES

*In this lesson we discover how the Bible's silence about the Church
in the Tribulation period is strong evidence for the Rapture.*

It's time to dive deep into the book of Revelation to discover what Jesus
has to say to His Church on earth—and why He suddenly has nothing
more to say to them after the third chapter. What does it mean that the
Church is given no instruction or encouragement as John lays out his
terrifying vision of future events? Are we going to be left to fend for ourselves as the world crumbles around us? Or is this silence a powerful clue
to a very different kind of future?

OUTLINE

   I. **Dead Silence About the Presence of the Church**

  II. **Dead Silence About the Preparation of the Church**

 III. **Dead Silence About the Purpose of the Church**

OVERVIEW

Sherlock Holmes is history's favorite detective. As we all know, he solved his cases by noticing what others missed. Remember the story of the dog that didn't bark? It started when a famous racehorse named Silver Blaze disappeared the night before the race. Then came the murder of the horse's trainer. Holmes investigated, and when a Scotland Yard inspector asked him what had caught his attention, he answered, "The curious incident of the dog in the nighttime."

"The dog did nothing in the nighttime," said the inspector.

"That was the curious incident," replied Sherlock.

Because the watchdog didn't bark, Holmes deduced the culprit was not a stranger to the dog, but someone the dog recognized. He called this a "negative fact," and he later said he solved the case when he "grasped the significance of the silence of the dog."[1]

There are many times when silence is a powerful witness to the facts, and that's true when it comes to the Rapture of the Church and the events of the Tribulation as we find them in the book of Revelation. We've already established our conviction that the Rapture occurs before the Tribulation. The "curious incident" of dead silence regarding the Church in the core chapters of Revelation comes alongside that conclusion and helps corroborate it.

Dead Silence About the Presence of the Church

Many of us who study the book of Revelation have found it to be one of the best organized books in the Bible. One particular verse in the first chapter gives us an outline of the entire book. The first half of the first chapter is the prologue, and the last part of Revelation 1 is John's initial vision of the glorified Jesus, who tells him in verse 19: "Write the things which you have seen, and the things which are, and the things which will take place after this."

This is God's own framework to the book of Revelation.

The things which you have seen. That's the first chapter and John's incredible opening vision of Jesus. John was on the island of Patmos in exile. He heard the blast of a trumpet and turned to see the glorious figure of the enthroned Christ, whom he described in magnificent detail. Christ spoke and explained the meaning of the symbols surrounding Him. The Lord told John to write down this opening vision he had seen.

The things which are. This refers to the next two chapters, Revelation 2–3, which contain seven short messages to the seven churches of Asia Minor. John oversaw these churches as an elder in exile. Each message describes the spiritual health of a given church, accompanied by commendations, reprimands, warnings, and rebukes. These messages are applicable throughout the entire age of the Church, and they are important for us today.

The things which will take place after this. This refers to the core chapters of Revelation, which begin with Revelation 4 and continue through the end of the book. These chapters detail the events that will take place in the future. Almost everything in Revelation 4–18 has to do with the seven-year Tribulation, describing in great detail the pouring out of God's wrath upon the earth. Chapter 19 is devoted to the Second Coming of Christ at the end of the Tribulation.

Do you know what is conspicuously absent from these Tribulation chapters? The Church. The word "church" appears nineteen times in Revelation 1–3 but not once in Revelation 4–18. Why the silence? Because the Church will no longer be on the earth. Believers will be removed before the Tribulation period and taken to heaven by means of the Rapture.

Notice how the account of the Tribulation begins unfolding in Revelation 4. Verse 1 says, "After these things I looked, and behold, a door standing open in heaven. And the first voice which I heard was like a trumpet speaking with me, saying, 'Come up here, and I will show you things which must take place after this.' "

We shouldn't base our opinions about the Rapture of the Church on a single verse, but since we have studied the primary Rapture passages already, it's hard not to see some similarities. We have what Sherlock Holmes would call a meaningful clue. Actually, several meaningful clues.

To start, we see John confronted by heaven through the means of an open door. There is even the possibility that John was drawn up to heaven—that he experienced a precursor to the Rapture in the same way as Enoch and Elijah and Paul. When did that happen? After "these things," which refers to the message John received for the churches in chapters 2 and 3.

Next, not only did John see an open door, but he also heard a voice like a trumpet. The great Rapture passages in 1 Thessalonians and 1 Corinthians both refer to the blast of a trumpet. In addition, John heard the command, "Come up here," which must surely be similar if not identical to the shout Jesus will give when He comes for us at the Rapture.

The clues offered to us in the first verse of Revelation 4 point strongly to the conclusion that John's experiences were a preview of the Rapture. John Strombeck affirmed that idea without pressing the point out of proportion when he wrote, "No event recorded in Revelation can better represent the Rapture of the church" than John's being caught up to heaven in Revelation 4:1.[2]

One phrase is repeated seven times in Revelation 2 and 3 at the conclusion of each of Christ's messages to His seven churches. That phrase is a convicting command: "He who has an ear, let him hear what the Spirit says to the churches" (2:7, 11, 17, 29; 3:6, 13, 22). No similar phrase occurs again in Revelation until we come to chapter 13, the midpoint in the Tribulation when the Antichrist rises in all his demonic power to terrorize the world. At that point, we read in Revelation 13:9: "If anyone has an ear, let him hear." What's missing? The writer no longer says, "What the Spirit says to the churches." Why? Because the Church is no longer around.[3]

To summarize, the Church is on earth in Revelation 1–3, then there is no record of anything being done by the Church in chapters 4–18. Evangelism is carried out by 144,000 Jewish evangelists. The action centers around the nation of Israel. The Spirit says nothing to the Church during these terrible years, for the Church is in heaven. Only when we get to the account of the Second Coming of Christ in chapter 19 do we see Him coming with His people—the "armies in heaven" (Revelation 19:14).

Dead Silence About the Preparation of the Church

Here's something else to think about: The New Testament is full of instructions for the Church. In fact, from the first chapter of Romans until the fourth chapter of Revelation, the primary emphasis of the New Testament writers involves how we, as Christians on earth, should conduct ourselves.

We're told about our morality, our theology, our faith, our behavior, our mission. We're even told how to react to the tribulations of life that we must endure. But those instructions suddenly stop when we come to Revelation 4. There are no specific instructions given to the Church in Revelation 4–18.

What's more, there's not a single passage in the New Testament that says something like, "During the Great Tribulation, here is what you should do. Here is how you should behave." If it were our lot to endure the wrath that will devastate the earth during those seven years, isn't it odd God never gave us one tidbit of information, encouragement, warning, or instruction on our preparation for it? The apostolic writers are strangely muted in giving any counsel to the Church regarding our behavior during the Tribulation. The reason for that omission is clear. The Church will not be present at all when the Tribulation takes place.

Richard Mayhue writes, "It would be inconsistent for the Scriptures to be silent on such a traumatic change for the church. If any time of the Rapture other than the pretribulational were true, one would expect the Epistles to teach the fact of the church in the tribulation, the purpose of the church in the tribulation, the conduct of the church in the tribulation. However there is no teaching like this whatsoever. Only a pretribulation rapture satisfactorily explains such obvious silence."[4]

Dead Silence About the Purpose of the Church

Likewise, there is no account of the Church's purpose during the Tribulation because the Church has no purpose in the Tribulation. The Tribulation period marks the final application of God's wrath upon Israel's transgressions, as we read in Ezekiel 20:37–38. God's wrath is reserved for apostate Israel—for those He nurtured and cherished and yet who departed from Him. The Tribulation period is essentially a family matter between Israel and God.

It's also a time when God will bring judgment upon all the evil that's being perpetuated in and on the earth. The purpose of the Tribulation is to execute God's wrath on those who reject Him, and that helps us understand why He would want to get the Church out of the way and to a place of safety—to a heavenly refuge where we'll be protected from that wrath. By simple logic, then, we can see why believers are to be spared the Tribulation. What would be the point of having to endure it? By turning to God for salvation, our rebellion has been forgiven, and we have no need to be purged of it or punished for it.

In fact, the Bible clearly tells us that our salvation is a salvation from God's wrath. The apostle Paul wrote in his Rapture-rich book of 1 Thessalonians that we're "to wait for His Son from heaven, whom He raised from the dead, even Jesus who delivers us from the wrath to come. . . . For God did not appoint us to wrath, but to obtain salvation through our Lord Jesus Christ" (1 Thessalonians 1:10; 5:9). Romans 5:9 makes the same point: "Much more then, having now been justified by His blood, we shall be saved from wrath through Him." Oh, our merciful Christ!

When God put Jesus on the Cross, He exacted from Him the full penalty due for our sin. We have nothing left to pay. Accordingly, if we who have been cleansed by the blood of Jesus were to be put through the Tribulation—a time of punitive judgment from God—it would mean the price Christ paid on the Cross was not enough. It would mean we still need the additional penalty of God's judicial wrath. The whole idea undermines the sufficiency of Christ's sacrifice for our sins.

Let me quote John Strombeck again: "One is forced to ask, how could the Lamb of God die and rise again to save the church from wrath and then allow her to pass through the wrath that He shall pour out upon those who reject Him? Such inconsistency might be possible in the thinking of men, but not in the acts of the Son of God."[5]

Dr. Tim Lahaye agreed:

> I simply cannot imagine the heavenly Bridegroom whispering to His chosen one: "Yes, My bride, My precious one, I love you so much that I gave My life for you. I want to nourish and cherish you. I want to take you home with Me and celebrate our marriage with joy and singing and feasting. I want to be with you forever. But before I bring you Home, I want you to experience seven years of the very fury of hell, and seven years of the terrible wrath of My Father. But try not to worry. I'll come back when it's all over."[6]

Our Lord and Savior will not be so cavalier with the people He died to save. Not with His Bride. Instead, He will rescue us from the coming wrath and cherish us for eternity.

APPLICATION

Personal Questions

1. Describe a time in your life when silence was more powerful than words.

2. Read Revelation 1:19.

    a. What are the three major sections of the book of Revelation?

    b. In which chapters does the word "church" not appear?

3. Read Revelation 4:1. What clues in this verse point to the Rapture of the Church before the Tribulation period?

4. What specific instructions do the New Testament writers give to the Church regarding our behavior during the Tribulation?

5. What is the purpose of the Tribulation?

6. Read 1 Thessalonians 5:9 and Romans 5:9. What is God's purpose and plan for believers?

7. What can you do to lovingly warn your unbelieving loved ones, acquaintances, and neighbors about God's righteous judgment during the Tribulation?

Group Questions

1. Discuss why silence can sometimes be more powerful than words.

2. Read Revelation 1:19 together and discuss the three major sections of Revelation.

   a. Where does the word "church" not appear in the book of Revelation?

b. How is this evidence that the Church will not go through the Tribulation period?

3. Read Revelation 4:1 and discuss the clues found in this verse that point to the Rapture of the Church before the Tribulation.

4. Do the New Testament writers give specific instructions to the Church regarding our behavior during the Tribulation? Why or why not?

5. Read 1 Thessalonians 5:9 and Romans 5:9. Discuss what these verses tell us about God's purpose and plan for believers.

6. Share with the group ways you can lovingly warn your unbelieving loved ones, acquaintances, and neighbors about God's righteous judgment that will come during the Tribulation.

DID YOU KNOW?

When Paul wrote, "Much more then, having now been justified by His blood, we shall be saved from wrath through Him" (Romans 5:9), he used a Greek idiom that was common in the writing of that time. The thought behind the phrase "much more" is "from the heavier to the lighter." In other words, God has done the harder thing in dying for us when we were enemies. Will He not do the easier thing in living for us now that we are His friends? If God has loved us when we were sinners, how could He let us endure the Tribulation now that we are His children?

Notes

1. Arthur Conan Doyle, *The Memoirs of Sherlock Holmes*, vol. 1 (Leipzig: Bernhard Tauchnitz, 1894), 50, 58.
2. J. F. Strombeck, *First the Rapture: The Church's Blessed Hope* (Grand Rapids, MI: Kregel, 1992), 185–186.
3. Tim LaHaye, *No Fear of the Storm* (Sisters, OR: Multnomah Press, 1992), 45–46.
4. Richard Mayhue, "Why a Pretribulation Rapture?," in *Christ's Prophetic Plans: A Futuristic Premillenial Primer*, ed. John Macarthur and Richard Mayhue (Chicago, IL: Moody Publishers, 2012), 91.
5. J. F. Strombeck, *First the Rapture: The Church's Blessed Hope* (Grand Rapids, MI: Kregel, 1992), 133.
6. Tim LaHaye, *No Fear of the Storm* (Sisters OR: Multnomah Press, 1992), 57.

RAPTURE AND RETURN

TITUS 2:13

*In this lesson we learn about the key differences between
the Rapture and the Second Coming.*

One of the biggest questions we have about the future is this: Will the
Rapture and the Second Coming of Christ happen at the same
time? Or are these two distinct events? And, if we're honest, we have many
more questions! What does it mean for believers if these two events
don't happen at the same time? Why does it matter that I understand this
at all? What difference could it make in my life and my witness?

OUTLINE

I. Different Settings

II. Different Signals

III. **Different Scripts**

IV. **Different Spectators**

OVERVIEW

Did you know a mix-up in terms once cost the U.S. government more than $150 million? In 1999, NASA launched a new Mars orbiter toward the Red Planet. After a journey of 286 days, the orbiter was poised to fire one final engine burst in order to establish a stable orbit around Mars. The engines did fire but not correctly. The orbiter pushed too close to the planet and was slung by gravity back into space, where it became lost.

What happened? After an extensive review, NASA engineers determined that some of the orbiter's navigation commands were programmed by the manufacturer using standard American units—inches, feet, miles, and so on. That caused a problem because all of NASA's programs and instructions were based on the metric system. Lorell Young, at the time president of the U.S. Metric Association, summarized the issue succinctly: "In this day and age when the metric system is the measurement language of all sophisticated science, two measurement systems should not be used."[1]

Mix-ups in terminology can be harmful in any field, including our study of biblical prophecy and the End Times. One particular misunderstanding that occurs regularly and often hinders the way people grasp God's prophetic plan is confusing the Rapture and the Second Coming. Many who read Scripture lump these two occurrences into the same moment—they think of Christians being caught up in the Rapture even as Christ descends from heaven to bring judgment on the earth. In reality, these are two separate terms that describe two distinct events.

As we'll see, there are many similarities between the Rapture and the Second Coming, and so the confusion is understandable. But in order to have a firm grasp of God's prophetic plan for the future, we need to notice the distinctions between these two events. Let's dig deeper by exploring four notable differences that will help us separate these two appearances of Christ.

Different Settings

The Rapture and the Second Coming will take place at different chronological times and in separate geographical places. They have different settings.

The Rapture is the first event in the prophetic content of the book of Revelation, and it is the next event on God's eschatological calendar. It is the opening salvo of the End Times. We don't know when the Rapture will occur—no person knows the day or the hour. Yet the signs of the times seem to indicate it will be coming soon.

On the other hand, we do know when the Second Coming will take place: seven years after the Rapture. Only then will Christ descend from His throne to inhabit our world once again in a physical way.

Here's another question that sometimes puzzles students of biblical prophecy: Since Christ will return to call up His saints in the Rapture and since the Rapture precedes the Second Coming, why is it called the Second Coming? Shouldn't it be the Third Coming?

The answer has to do with the physical locations of those two events. When Christ reenters our world at the Second Coming, He will begin that process in the atmosphere. As John wrote in Revelation: "Look, he is coming with the clouds, and every eye will see him, even those who pierced him. And all the tribes of the earth will mourn over him. So it is to be. Amen" (1:7 csb).

Once He has alerted the world to His presence, Christ will continue His descent and alight on very specific geographical coordinates: the Mount of Olives. Remember the words of the angels after Jesus ascended into heaven: "They were looking intently up into the sky as he was going, when suddenly two men dressed in white stood beside them. 'Men of Galilee,' they said, 'why do you stand here looking into the sky? This same Jesus, who has been taken from you into heaven, will come back in the same way you have seen him go into heaven'" (Acts 1:10–11 niv).

The prophet Zechariah was boldly specific in his promises about that future moment. "On that day his feet will stand on the Mount of Olives, east of Jerusalem, and the Mount of Olives will be split in two from east to west, forming a great valley, with half of the mountain moving north and half moving south" (Zechariah 14:4 niv).

Christ's return at the Rapture will also begin in the atmosphere, but it will not progress to the ground. The dead in Christ will rise first at that moment, and then "we who are still alive and are left will be caught up together with them in the clouds to meet the Lord in the air. And so we will be with the Lord forever" (1 Thessalonians 4:17 NIV).

Different Signals

There will be no specific signs that signal the approach of the Rapture. Scripture is clear, and that moment will come "like a thief in the night" (1 Thessalonians 5:2 NIV). Jesus told us, "Two men will be in the field: one will be taken and the other left. Two women will be grinding at the mill: one will be taken and the other left. Watch therefore, for you do not know what hour your Lord is coming" (Matthew 24:40–42).

The Second Coming is different. That event will be preceded by several signs that are well-defined and impossible to miss.

Of course, the first concrete sign for the Second Coming will be the Rapture itself! Christ's return to gather His Church—first those who have died, then those who are alive at that moment—will be the catalyst that initiates the Tribulation. For three-and-a-half years, the Antichrist will consolidate power and draw the nations of the world together into a single system, a single government under the direct control of Satan.

Then, to borrow a common phrase, all hell will break loose. The final three-and-a-half years of the Tribulation period are often called the Great Tribulation. This will be a season of wars and rumors of wars, of pestilence and plague, of apostasy and persecution—all on a scale previously unimaginable in human history.

At the end of the Great Tribulation, the armies of the nations will assemble on the fields outside Megiddo in Israel. The purpose of those armies will be direct confrontation not only with Israel as a nation but also with God Himself. The majority of humanity will align with Satan and the Antichrist in unmitigated rebellion against the living God.

And the living God will respond. The doors of heaven will be opened, and Christ will appear in full glory.

I saw heaven standing open and there before me was a white horse, whose rider is called Faithful and True. With justice he judges and wages war. His eyes are like blazing fire, and on his head are many crowns. He has a name written on him that no one knows but he himself. He is dressed in a robe dipped in blood, and his name is the Word of God. The armies of heaven were following him, riding on white horses and dressed in fine linen, white and clean. Coming out of his mouth is a sharp sword with which to strike down the nations. "He will rule them with an iron scepter." He treads the winepress of the fury of the wrath of God Almighty (Revelation 19:11–15 NIV).

Different Scripts

We have clear teaching from the Bible that Jesus does not change. He is "the same yesterday, today, and forever" (Hebrews 13:8). Yet there does seem to be a sense in which Jesus operates in different roles when He interacts with our world at specific times. He emphasizes different elements of His character depending on the script or mission of the moment.

The Gospels primarily portray Jesus as the Lamb of God slain to cover the sins of the world. He is the Suffering Servant—the living personification of God's prophecies in Isaiah 53. Of course, Jesus also operated as a Rabbi, teaching us in both word and deed what we need to know as His followers. But His main task was to rescue His people from their sin. He came as our Savior.

At the Second Coming, Jesus will operate from a much different role. He will return as the Conquering King, the Lion of Judah. Riding on His white horse and adorned with a robe dipped in blood, the One we know as Christ will reenter our world as the living personification of God's judgment and wrath against sin.

But there's a third role outlined for Jesus in the Scriptures: the Bridegroom of the Church (see Matthew 25:1–13). This is the script Jesus will primarily follow at the Rapture. In that brief moment, He will return not as a sacrifice nor as a conqueror but as the Lover of our souls.

Different Spectators

The Rapture and the Second Coming of Christ are two distinct events that will occur in different settings, be preceded by different signals, and follow different scripts. Here's another distinction—they will be observed by different spectators.

During the Rapture, only those who have accepted the salvation of Jesus Christ will be aware of His presence. He will appear only to His Bride, the Church. Of course, the rest of the world will see the *effects* of the Rapture—they will notice the huge number of people who literally disappeared in an instant—but they won't understand the cause. In this way, Jesus will function as a "special ops" soldier at the Rapture. He will gather believers as part of a secret, quick-hitting rescue mission.

That will not be the case at the Second Coming. Rather than operating in stealth, Christ will return in splendor—and everyone will see. Remember Revelation 1:7, which promises: "Look, he is coming with the clouds, and every eye will see him, even those who pierced him. And all the tribes of the earth will mourn over him. So it is to be. Amen" (CSB).

Similarly, the experience for Christians during the Rapture will be primarily passive. Believers both living and dead will be "caught up," but all the action will be taken by Christ. We will be more involved at the Second Coming. When John foresaw Jesus bursting through the heavenly gates on His white horse, "the armies of heaven were following him, riding on white horses and dressed in fine linen, white and clean" (Revelation 19:14 NIV). That's us. You and me. We will actively join the armies of God in retaking this world for His Kingdom.

One fascinating aspect of these truths is that there will be a generation of Jesus-followers who will experience both the Rapture and the Second Coming within their lifetimes. These women and men will be alive at the moment of the Rapture, which means they will be caught up with Christ. Then, seven years later on earth, they will return with Christ as members of His heavenly host. What a gift to experience such a double blessing! And what a reminder that the Rapture and the Second Coming are both out-workings of the Gospel.

There has been a tendency throughout history to think of end times events as bad news—as the end of something helpful that we wish would keep going. This is not the case! The Rapture and the Second Coming are both important steps that must be taken to initiate the next phase of our life: eternity. But it helps to come to terms with the terms, doesn't it? He is coming again in no uncertain terms!

Vance Havner said, "When I studied arithmetic, I remembered that the answers were in the back of the book. No matter how I floundered among my problems, the correct solution was on the last page."[2] Our world is floundering with many problems today, but the answers we need are on the Bible's last page. " 'Surely I am coming quickly.' Amen. Even so, come, Lord Jesus!" (Revelation 22:20).

APPLICATION

Personal Questions

1. Describe a particular time when a failure to define terms resulted in a disagreement or misunderstanding.

2. List the four notable differences between the Rapture and the Second Coming.

3. Where will the Second Coming take place? Where will the Rapture take place? How do we know?

4. What signs will precede the Rapture? What signs will precede the Second Coming?

5. Read Revelation 19:11–15. How will Jesus appear at His Second Coming?

6. Explain how Jesus interacts with the world at the following times:

    a. In the Gospels

    b. At the Rapture

    c. At His Second Coming

7. What "double blessing" could be available to you today?

8. How can you personally keep your excitement about the Rapture and the Second Coming from growing cold?

Group Questions

1. Discuss how important it is to define your terms when communicating with another person.

2. Discuss the four notable differences between the Rapture and the Second Coming.

3. Explain where the Rapture will take place and where the Second Coming will take place. What Scripture verses give us this information?

4. The Rapture and the Second Coming have different signs. List the signs for each below.

   a. Rapture

   b. Second Coming

5. Read Revelation 19:11–15 together and discuss how Jesus will appear at His Second Coming.

6. Discuss Jesus' different roles as found in the Gospels, at the Rapture, and at the Second Coming. What do these roles teach us about Jesus?

7. How can you help each other stay excited about the Rapture and the Second Coming?

DID YOU KNOW?

Even today, the location of Christ's Second Coming—the Mount of Olives—offers one of the most breathtaking views in the world, especially when the morning sun casts its glow across the golden city with its haunting walls, limestone buildings, ancient monuments, steeples, spires, and minarets. Interestingly, many of the slopes of the Mount of Olives are now covered with concrete tombs. Faithful Jews want to be buried there so they'll be close at hand when the long awaited Messiah arrives to enter the Eastern Gate of Jerusalem. No one knows how many people are buried there, but the number may reach 150,000.[3]

Notes
1. Robin Lloyd, "Metric Mishap Caused Loss of NASA Orbiter," CNN, September 30, 1999, http://www.cnn.com/TECH/space/9909/30/mars.metric.02/.
2. Vance Havner, "Second Coming of Christ—Quotes, Devotionals & Illustrations," Precept Austin, https://www.preceptaustin.org/second_coming_of_christ.
3. "Mount of Olives," Tourist Israel: The Guide, August 16, 2023, https://www.touristisrael.com/mount-of-olives/27213/#:~:text=Today%2C%20the%20Mount%20of%20Olives,the%20most%20prominent%20biblical%20kings.

SHOCK AND AWE

MATTHEW 24:27, 29–30

In this lesson we learn about the central doctrines relating to the Second Coming of Christ.

OUTLINE

The arrival of the longed-for Messiah for the Jewish people will happen one day—His feet will land on the Mount of Olives, splitting it in two. What some people, including the prophets of old, did not fully understand is that there are two separate events—the first coming and the second coming. None of us were present for His first coming, but when He returns the second time, all the saints will return with Him and participate in the battle to reclaim the world.

I. The Priority of the Second Coming

II. The Prophecies of the Second Coming

III. The Purpose of the Second Coming

IV. **The Participants in the Second Coming**

V. **The Punishment at the Second Coming**

OVERVIEW

A young couple began searching for a new, bigger apartment after the birth of their first child. As residents of Jerusalem, they were used to tight spaces, so finding the right place to live would be a challenge. They found a place that was a perfect fit, but as they prepared to sign the lease, they saw this provision: "Upon the coming of the Messiah, tenants agree to vacate the apartment within fifteen days."[1] The apartment had a Messiah clause.

You won't find that sentence on legal documents in America, but when Jewish homeowners rent their property in Jerusalem, they often include a clause that ensures they will be able to return and reign with the Messiah should He appear during their lifetime. Jews believe that when the Messiah sets foot in Jerusalem it will be for the first time. Christians understand that *Mashiach*—the Hebrew term for Messiah—already came and ultimately ascended into heaven from its highest hill after His resurrection.

These conflicting views of the Messiah's return originated with the Old Testament prophets who did not view the first and second advents as separate events. They saw both comings of Christ either as one event or very closely related in time. Even Jesus' followers expected Him to fulfill the glorious promises relating to His Second Coming when He came the first time. It was only after He ascended to heaven that they realized that they were living in the time between His two appearances.

The Priority of the Second Coming

While Christians are most familiar with the first coming of Christ, it is the Second Coming of Christ that gets the most attention in the Bible. References to the Second Coming outnumber references to the first coming by a factor of eight to one. The Second Coming is second only to salvation as the most dominant subject in the New Testament. The fact that Christ's

Second Coming features so prominently in Scripture is an indication that this event is important to God—and that it should be important to us as well.

The Prophecies of the Second Coming

Here are seven key passages that predict the return of our Lord to the earth, spanning from Enoch in Genesis to John in the book of Revelation.

Enoch: According to Jude, Enoch was the first to predict the Second Coming of Christ. "Now Enoch, the seventh from Adam, prophesied about these men also, saying, 'Behold, the Lord comes with ten thousands of His saints, to execute judgment on all, to convict all who are ungodly among them of all their ungodly deeds which they have committed in an ungodly way, and of all the harsh things which ungodly sinners have spoken against Him'" (Jude 14–15).

Daniel: Known for his prophetic dreams, both about events in his lifetime and things that will occur during the End Times, Daniel describes the return of the Son of Man. "I was watching in the night visions, and behold, One like the Son of Man, coming with the clouds of heaven! He came to the Ancient of Days, and they brought Him near before Him. Then to Him was given dominion and glory and a kingdom, that all peoples, nations, and languages should serve Him. His dominion is an everlasting dominion, which shall not pass away, and His kingdom the one which shall not be destroyed" (Daniel 7:13–14).

Zechariah: Zechariah deals in specifics, even pinpointing the geographic location to which Christ will return. "In that day His feet will stand on the Mount of Olives" (Zechariah 14:4). The Mount of Olives is an explicitly identifiable place that retains its ancient name even today.

Jesus: From the Mount of Olives, Jesus affirmed His Second Coming to His disciples in dramatic terms. He said, "For as the lightning comes from the east and flashes to the west, so also will the coming of the Son of Man be . . . . Immediately after the tribulation of those days the sun will be darkened, and the moon will not give its light; the stars will fall from heaven, and the powers of the heavens will be shaken. Then the sign of the Son of Man will appear in heaven, and then all the tribes of the earth will mourn, and they will see the Son of Man coming on the clouds of heaven with power and great glory" (Matthew 24:27, 29–30).

The two angels: Immediately following Christ's ascension into heaven, two angels appeared to the disciples and spoke words of comfort to them. They said, "Men of Galilee, why do you stand gazing up into heaven? This same Jesus, who was taken up from you into heaven, will so come in like manner as you saw Him go into heaven" (Acts 1:11). The next verse tells us, "They returned to Jerusalem from the mount called Olivet" (verse 12). Jesus ascended to heaven from the Mount of Olives. According to the angels, Jesus will return to the very same spot—the Mount of Olives. The words of the angels conveyed both consolation for their present loss and confirmation of His future return. The time of our Lord's return is uncertain (see Matthew 24:36), but when that day comes, all eyes will be fixed on the sky above the Mount of Olives.

Paul: In 2 Thessalonians, Paul describes what the Day of Judgment will be like. "The Lord Jesus is revealed from heaven with His mighty angels, in flaming fire taking vengeance on those who do not know God, and on those who do not obey the gospel of our Lord Jesus Christ. These shall be punished with everlasting destruction from the presence of the Lord and from the glory of His power, when He comes, in that Day, to be glorified in His saints and to be admired among all those who believe, because our testimony among you was believed" (1:7–10).

John: The prophecies of Christ's return are like bookends to Revelation. In the first chapter John wrote, "Behold, He is coming with clouds, and every eye will see Him, even they who pierced Him. And all the tribes of the earth will mourn because of Him" (verse 7). And in the second to final verse of Revelation our Lord emphatically affirms His Second Coming. "He who testifies to these things says, 'Surely I am coming quickly.' Amen. Even so, come, Lord Jesus!" (22:20).

The Purpose of the Second Coming

During the 2003 invasion of Iraq, a military strategy called "shock and awe" was employed. "Shock and awe" is a sudden, overwhelming display of military force which can paralyze the enemy's perception of the battlefield and destroy their desire to fight.

When Jesus leads His heavenly offensive against Satan and the Antichrist at the Battle of Armageddon, He will follow a similar strategy.

In that final showdown, the rebellion of the Tribulation period will come to an end. The Antichrist, the kings of the earth, and the souls that follow them will gather one last time to try to defeat Jesus Christ. Their armies will be made up of soldiers from the ten nations of the revived Roman Empire. The Beast (the Antichrist) with the False Prophet at his side will lead those massive armies in defying Christ's authority and right to rule—the ultimate revolt against God. When Christ's return draws near, they will do everything they can to prepare for the battle of the ages. And they will fail miserably.

The apostle John describes this moment: "Behold, he is coming with clouds, and every eye will see Him, even they who pierced Him. And all the tribes of the earth will mourn because of Him" (Revelation 1:7).

Jesus came the first time in obscurity and simplicity, but the second time He will come in glory and majesty, shining forth in victory. It will bring the world to its knees. According to John, "His eyes were like a flame of fire, and on His head were many crowns. He had a name written that no one knew except Himself. He was clothed with a robe dipped in blood, and His name is called The Word of God" (Revelation 19:12–13).

First, Jesus' eyes are flames of fire as He gazes upon the hearts and minds of mankind. This signifies the Lord's ability to see deeply into the hearts of men and deal with all injustice (see Revelation 1:14; 2:18; 19:12). His eyes will pierce through the motives of nations and individuals and judge them for what they really are.

Second, the head of the returning Christ is crowned with many crowns. When He came the first time, they mocked Him and placed a crown of thorns on His head. When He comes again, His crowns symbolize that no rule, might, or authority will be able to stand against Him.

Third, Jesus' robe being dipped in blood speaks of the redemption He secured for us on the Cross. He is the Lamb that was slain (see Revelation 13:8). For all eternity we will celebrate the shed blood which purchased our redemption from the penalty of sin.

As Christ leads His armies in victory, a name is written on His thigh: "KING OF KINGS AND LORD OF LORDS" (Revelation 19:16). Of all the kings on earth, He is the King. Of all earthly lords (rulers, those in authority), He is the Lord. Every knee will bow when He comes to earth (see Isaiah 45:23; Romans 14:11; Philippians 2:10–11).

The Participants in the Second Coming

"And the armies in heaven, clothed in fine linen, white and clean, followed Him on white horses" (Revelation 19:14).

When Christ returns, He will bring His armies as part of His shock-and-awe campaign. Note the word in verse 14 is "armies," plural. It is not the "army" of heaven but the "armies." These armies are the believers from all of time: the Old Testament saints, the New Testament saints, and the Tribulation saints. All the many legions of our Lord will be combined into one massive army.

Zechariah wrote, "The Lord my God will come, and all the holy ones with him" (Zechariah 14:5 NIV). In his letters to the Thessalonians, Paul spoke of the saints who would accompany the Lord when He returned: "So that He may establish your hearts blameless in holiness before our God and Father at the coming of our Lord Jesus Christ with all His saints" (1 Thessalonians 3:13).

Jude echoed the same idea: "Listen! The Lord is coming with countless thousands of his holy ones" (verse 14 NLT). All those who have died in the Lord, along with those who were raptured before the years of the Tribulation, will return with Christ and participate in the battle to reclaim the world for the rule of Christ. They will be dressed in white linen, representing the righteousness of those who have been saved by the blood of the Lamb. Jesus will be clothed in a blood-stained garment so that we might wear the white linen of His righteousness.

But the saints are not the only armies of our Lord. Matthew tells us that the angels will also descend with Christ. "When the Son of Man comes in His glory, and all the holy angels with Him, then He will sit on the throne of His glory" (Matthew 25:31). And Paul said, "When the Lord Jesus is revealed from heaven with His mighty angels" (2 Thessalonians 1:7).

The Punishment at the Second Coming

In Revelation 19:11, we are given the central purpose for Christ's return to the earth: "In righteousness He judges and makes war." Jesus will come as the Judge of all things—including all people.

Jude describes the world that Christ will find when He returns. "Behold, the Lord comes with ten thousands of His saints, to execute judgment on all, to convict all who are ungodly among them of all their ungodly deeds which they have committed in an ungodly way, and of all the harsh things which ungodly sinners have spoken against Him" (Jude 14–15). Jude used the word "ungodly" four times. This repetition is not accidental. When Christ returns, He will come to impose judgment on the "ungodly," including the Antichrist and his False Prophet who will be "cast alive into the lake of fire burning with brimstone" (Revelation 19:20–21). Satan will join them after the Millennium—"And they will be tormented day and night forever and ever" (Revelation 20:10).

Why the wrath and judgment of God? A good God must be a God of judgment. At the time God has ordained, Jesus will descend from heaven and crush the evil forces that have invaded this world—restoring His rightful rule over the earth—KING OF KINGS AND LORD OF LORDS!

APPLICATION

Personal Questions

1. Have you ever met someone who is still waiting for the Messiah to come? If so, what Scriptures did you use to show that the Messiah has already come the first time? If you have never encountered someone who is still waiting for the Messiah, take the time now to record some of the verses that clearly show He has already come and will come again.

2. Why is the Second Coming a priority?

3. Read Daniel 7:13–14. Write down the key points that are found in Daniel's prophecy that are relevant to us today.

4. Read Matthew 24:27–30 and Zechariah 14:4. What role does the Mount of Olives play in these verses?

5. Under the section, "The Purpose of the Second Coming," the two arrivals of Christ are contrasted. Write down how they will differ.

    a. First Coming

    b. Second Coming

6. Those that return with Christ will have white garments while His robe will be "dipped in blood" (Revelation 19:13). What significance is found in the apparel that will be worn on that day?

7. Read Jude 14–15.

    a. Who will come with Christ when He returns?

    b. What will Christ find when He returns, and how will He respond?

Group Questions

1. Discuss the following questions as a group.

   a. Have you ever had questions about whether the Messiah would come only once?

   b. After studying this lesson, do you feel better equipped to discuss why the Messiah has already come and will come again at some time in the future?

2. Together read Daniel 7:13–14. Discuss the key points in Daniel's prophecy that are relevant to us today as we await Christ's return.

3. Read Matthew 24:27–30 and Zechariah 14:4. Discuss the importance of the Mount of Olives and the role it will play in Christ's return.

4. Review the section, "The Purpose of the Second Coming," and then discuss how the two appearances of Christ on earth are different.

5. Read Revelation 19:11–13. What is the importance of what is revealed in those verses about Christ's eyes, head, and robe?

6. Read Jude 14–15 together. Discuss the state of the world when Christ returns. Who will return with Him, and how will He respond to the evil that has pervaded the earth?

7. Read Revelation 20:10. What is the fate of Satan, the False Prophet, and the Beast (the Antichrist) for the evil they have done to people?

DID YOU KNOW?

If you are among those who struggle with the thought of God's wrath and judgment, these words from N. T. Wright may give you understanding. "The word *judgment* carries negative overtones for a good many people in our liberal and postliberal world. We need to remind ourselves that throughout the Bible . . . God's coming judgment is a good thing, something to be celebrated, longed for, yearned over. It causes people to shout for joy and the trees of the field to clap their hands. In a world of systematic injustice, bullying, violence, arrogance, and oppression, the thought that there might come a day when the wicked are firmly put in their place and the poor and weak are given their due is the best news there can be. Faced with a world in rebellion, a world full of exploitation and wickedness, a good God *must* be a God of judgment."[2]

Notes
1. Jenna Rose Alpern, "A Rental Contract for the End of Days," *Times of Israel*, February 10, 2014, https://blogs.timesofisrael.com/only-in-israel/.
2. N. T. Wright, *Surprised by Hope* (New York, NY: Harper Colins, 2008), 137.

LIVE LIKE YOU WERE DYING

ROMANS 13:11–14

*In this lesson we learn how to overcome the distractions of the
world and to purposefully live each day for God.*

In Romans chapter 13, Paul offered instruction on how to live as we anticipate Christ's return—to be watchful, to fight the darkness, to pursue holy living, and to "put on the Lord Jesus Christ." As we reject the seductiveness of the world and invest our time and energy in our walk with God, we become His light in the world until He comes.

OUTLINE

I. **We Are to Watch Vigilantly**

II. **We Are to War Valiantly**
   A. Put off Darkness
   B. Put on the Light

III. **We Are to Walk Virtuously**
   A. Reject Public Sins
   B. Renounce Private Sins

IV. **We Are to Wait Victoriously**
   A. Put on Christ
   B. Make No Provision for the Flesh

OVERVIEW

"Live Like You Were Dying" was the title of a Tim McGraw hit song some years back. The lyrics spoke of loving deeper and speaking sweeter and giving forgiveness once denied. The final thought in the song went like this: "Someday I hope you get the chance to live like you were dying."[1]

The country singer hit a chord: the importance of living on purpose. Our call is to live with a sense of urgency based on something higher than the pursuit of pleasure—knowing Jesus Christ as our Savior and Lord.

If ever there was a time for the Church of God and the people of Christ to catch this sense of urgency, that time is now. In Romans 13:11–14, Paul wrote, "And do this, knowing the time, that now it is high time to awake out of sleep; for now our salvation is nearer than when we first believed. The night is far spent, the day is at hand. Therefore let us cast off the works of darkness, and let us put on the armor of light. Let us walk properly, as in the day, not in revelry and drunkenness, not in lewdness and lust, not in strife and envy. But put on the Lord Jesus Christ, and make no provision for the flesh, to fulfill its lusts."

During this time of urgency, we need to make every effort to resist the seductiveness of our culture and cling close to Christ—to live like we were dying.

We Are to Watch Vigilantly

"And do this, knowing the time, that now it is high time to awake out of sleep; for now our salvation is nearer than when we first believed. The night is far spent, the day is at hand" (Romans 13:11-12). There are five references to time in those two verses.

- "Knowing the time"
- "Now it is high time"
- "Our salvation is nearer"
- "Night is far spent"
- "The day is at hand"

It has always been important to understand the times. The Bible tells us we should be interested and aware of what's going on. But we are remarkably blind to the workings of the Holy Spirit in our life. We're hypnotized by the rhythm of life, as if this moment has no bearing on eternity and everything is going to continue as it always has been.

Some people scoff at the thought of the Bible predicting the future. Peter encountered these people. "Scoffers will come in the last days . . . saying, 'Where is the promise of His coming?'" (2 Peter 3:3-4) No matter what people may think, the return of Christ is certain. Not only is the Lord's coming certain, but it is also imminent. "And do this, knowing the time, that now it is high time to awake out of sleep; for now our salvation is nearer than when we first believed" (Romans 13:11).

The way Paul expressed this truth about our Lord's return in this passage causes some confusion—"For now our salvation is nearer than when we first believed" (Romans 13:11). If someone asks, "Do you know when Jesus is coming back?" You can reply, "Yes, He's coming back sooner than when I became a Christian."

When Paul used the word "salvation" here, he was seeing that concept in its completeness—in its fullness. The moment we say "Yes" to Christ, we are sealed by the Holy Spirit, our sins are washed away, and we are saved. The next thing that happens is we begin to grow and become more like Christ. We are being sanctified, being made holy. And when we stand before the Lord someday, we'll be made perfect and set free of every sin.

Salvation past, present and future—I have been saved from the penalty of sin, and I am being saved from the power of sin. Sanctification teaches us how to be victorious in our life. But ultimately, one day when I stand before the Lord there will be no sin in heaven. I will be saved from the presence of sin. And my salvation at that moment will be complete when Jesus takes me to Himself.

Paul was saying that when we are freed from the very presence of sin, when we stand in the presence of the Lord, that part of our salvation is nearer than when we believed. He was saying, "He's coming back, and His coming is nearer than when you became a Christian." It reminds us that we don't know when He will return.

The whole purpose of the Rapture is to inject into our spirit a sense of urgency. It's not about knowing what's going to happen in the future. It's about knowing what's going to happen so we can get our act together now. We're to watch vigilantly.

We Are to War Valiantly

Then the Bible says we're to war valiantly. Paul said, "The night is far spent, the day is at hand. Therefore let us cast off the works of darkness, and let us put on the armor of light" (Romans 13:12). Paul was warning us about getting caught up in the world; instead, we are to lay aside any distractions and put on His light so that we will be ready for His return.

Put off Darkness

The first step in our war against Satan is to put off darkness. "The night is far spent, the day is at hand. . . . Cast off the works of darkness" (Romans 13:12). When Paul said to put off darkness, he chose a decisive verb. It means "to deliberately, purposefully, significantly, and permanently put aside the things of darkness." Darkness is a term used in Scripture to describe the life that we lived before Christ came into our lives.

Ephesians 5:8 says, "For you were once darkness, but now you are light in the Lord. Walk as children of light." Paul tells us that since our Lord's return is imminent, we should not let the old nature have any inroad into our life. While Christ is accepted in a moment, sin remains our foe for a lifetime.

Many followers of Christ are surprised to discover that when they become Christians their old nature doesn't go away. Maybe you're among those who think that when you got saved your old nature was eradicated. But even after we become Christians, we still struggle with sin because of our old nature. When we become Christians, we have the Holy Spirit and a new nature. But we still carry the desire to sin, so we need to actively resist Satan and his enticements. Paul is saying, if you're a Christian, you still have the old nature and you need to put off the darkness. Darkness is simply the absence of light. When the light comes, the darkness is no longer present.

Put on the Light

When we are told to put on the light, Paul is using the New Testament picture of walking in fellowship with Jesus. John said, "If we walk in the light as He is in the light, we have fellowship with one another, and the blood of Jesus Christ His Son cleanses us from all sin" (1 John 1:7).

The world is filled with darkness, so let your light shine. Look for opportunities to share the love of Jesus with the people you interact with daily. Jesus is coming back, so every moment counts.

We Are to Walk Virtuously

"Let us walk properly, as in the day, not in revelry and drunkenness, not in lewdness and lust, not in strife and envy" (Romans 13:13). Paul was not writing to pagans; he was writing to the Roman Christians. And he was saying don't do these six things. The six sins here fall into two categories. The first three have to do with public disgrace: revelry, drunkenness, and lewdness. And the last three have to do with sins that can hide in the human heart before they are manifest in the light of day: lust, strife, and envy. All of them are understood to be sins of the night and opposed to what you are as a Christian. The things that he lists in this paragraph have no place in the life of a Christian.

Christians need to live for God. And we can't make an impact on this dark world if we're as dark as the world is. When Paul wrote to the Thessalonians, he said, "You are all sons of light and sons of the day. We are not of the night nor of darkness" (1 Thessalonians 5:5).

Reject Public Sins

Reject revelry and drunkenness and lewdness. You can be in many churches and just live like you never changed a thing when you became a Christian. But the Bible calls us to holiness—it calls us to reject public sins.

Renounce Private Sins

We're not only to reject public sins, but we're also to renounce the private ones of lust, strife, and envy. Even if we think no one sees, God sees and knows where our heart truly lies. Renounce the sins that pull your heart and mind away from the things of the Lord.

We Are to Wait Victoriously

And then Paul said to these Christians, "Put on the Lord Jesus Christ, and make no provision for the flesh, to fulfill its lusts" (Romans 13:14). Are you listening to Paul's message? Are you thinking that Paul's explanations and expectations are unreasonable? The strength we require is available through the Spirit of God, and the strategy is in the Word of God. Once we determine to live in expectation of our Lord's return, we can be confident of victory. We can't be confident if we're making concessions to the enemy.

Put on Christ

Finally, Paul concluded by saying to "put on the Lord Jesus Christ." What does it mean to put on Christ? Ray Stedman said it this way: "When I get up in the morning, I put on my clothes, intending them to be part of me all day, to go where I go and do what I do. They cover me and make me presentable to others. That is the purpose of clothes. In the same way, the apostle is saying to us, 'Put on Jesus Christ when you wake up in the morning. Make Him part of your life that day. Intend that He go with you everywhere you go, and that He act through you in everything you do. Call upon His resources. Live your life IN CHRIST.' "[2]

Every day when you get up say, "Lord, today, You and I are going into this dark world, and we're going to make a difference with the people we are around. We're going to show people the influence of Jesus Christ."

Make No Provision for the Flesh

We cannot allow ourselves any possibility to gratify our fleshly desires. Believers who have been saved out of addictive lifestyles should carefully consider Paul's words here. The strategy for victory is to avoid the situations that enabled your addiction. Don't put yourself in places where you'll be tempted. Be ruthless in putting those old habits to death. Do it pointedly, and do it permanently. If you want to make a difference, live your life in such a way that you will be proud to meet Him when He returns—walk in the light.

If you're struggling as a Christian and you're not living victoriously, the devil is gaining an advantage. It may be time to change your environment—to carefully review where and with whom you spend your time. Don't set yourself up for failure by staying in an environment that encourages you to do wrong. Find friends and small groups that encourage you to do right and lift your spirit and your life. When we become Christians, Christ comes to live in us, and we learn to be uncomfortable with everything that grieves Him. Knowing that Christ lives in you is the greatest motivation toward godliness that you'll ever have.

It is impossible to earn your salvation—it is the precious gift of God to us. But here's what the Bible says we are to do: "Live a life worthy of the calling you have received" (Ephesians 4:1 NIV). Think often about His death and His sacrifice for you. Live a life that's worthy of what Jesus did on the Cross. Jesus will return one day, and we need to avoid doing anything that will sully the splendor of that event. As followers of Christ, we should keep one watchful eye on the headlines and the other on the sky.

APPLICATION

Personal Questions

1. Write down the five references to time that are found in Romans 13:11–12.

2. What do these "time" references say to you about the urgency of the time we are living in today?

3. Read Romans 13:12. What does it mean to "cast off the works of darkness"?

4. Read 1 John 1:7. What does it mean to walk in fellowship with Jesus?

5. What instruction does Ephesians 5:8 give to the follower of Christ?

6. Read 1 Thessalonians 5:5. What does it mean to be "sons of light and sons of the day"?

7. How would you put Romans 13:14 into action in your life?

8. After completing this lesson, does the idea to "live like you were dying" give you greater purpose? If so, write down the changes you will make to ensure that you live each day with purpose.

Group Questions

1. Read Romans 13:11–12 together as a group. Then list the five mentions of "time" in those verses and discuss how they reveal the urgency of Christ's return.

2. Read Romans 13:12. Compare and contrast the use of darkness and light in this lesson.

3. Read 1 John 1:7 as a group. Discuss what Christian fellowship means today and what fellowship with Jesus means.

4. Together discuss what it means in practical terms to "put off darkness" and to "put on Christ."

5. As a group read and discuss Ephesians 4:1.

6. Discuss how living as if you were dying impacts your daily life as a Christian.

DID YOU KNOW?

Where and how we spend our time has a tremendous influence on our behavior and our thoughts. According to James Clear, "Every environment promotes some behaviors and prevents others. The key is to be in an environment that supports the results you want to achieve. The people and places that surround us fill our days with little cues and triggers that can make our habits easier to follow or harder to build. Are you fighting your environment to make change happen? Or does your environment make your new behavior effortless?"[3] Choose to walk and live in the light of Christ, forsaking the darkness and its enticements.

Notes

1. Tim McGraw, vocalist, "Live Like You Were Dying," words and music by James Timothy Nichols and Craig Michael Wiseman, track five on Tim McGraw, *Live Like You Were Dying*, Curb Records, 2004.
2. Ray Stedman, Expository Studies in Romans 9–16: From Guilt to Glory, vol. 2 (Waco, TX: Word, 1978), 136.
3. James Clear, "4 Reasonable Ways to Achieve Overnight Success," *James Clear*,

THE FINAL INVITATION

REVELATION 22:17

*In this lesson we learn about God's free offer
of eternal life to everyone.*

While some might say that Christianity is a religion of exclusive elitists who seem to take pleasure in telling people they're going to hell, nothing could be further from the truth. God has opened wide the door of salvation, and He does not desire that sinners die but that they repent and live. But one day the door will shut. And whatever conclusion a person has come to about the work and person of Jesus Christ will be their final decision. For some, that time comes on the day they die. For those living in the Last Days, that time could come at the Rapture. So what will your answer be? Your eternal life depends on it.

OUTLINE

I. Your Invitation Is Ready

II. Your Response Is Required

OVERVIEW

Belinda Luscombe recalled the time she lost a large sum of money by forgetting to claim stock options. "One day," she wrote, "I had $70,000 waiting to be claimed, and then about a month later when I realized I had forgotten to click on the 'exercise trade' button on my computer—poof!—the opportunity was gone." Belinda's first, panicked thought was how she could tell her husband about her mistake. Then, the weight of her situation began to fully press down. In her words:

> It's hard to describe the feeling exactly. I imagine you could replicate the effects by lying on the ground and having a friend drop a bowling ball on your abdomen from atop a stepladder. There's a little shock, some confusion, pain, nausea, and a profound wish that this had happened to somebody else. For a while, it hurts to breathe.

"I had made something," she wrote, "it was there, but through sheer incompetence, it was gone. And it was All. My. Fault."[1]

Can you imagine the gut-wrenching regret of losing tens of thousands of dollars from carelessness? But that pales in comparison to the soul-shattering terror of missing your opportunity to claim the eternal riches offered by Christ.

A moment is coming when our world will change "in the twinkling of an eye." The Lord Jesus will appear in the clouds and gather His people to Himself—first those who've died in Him, and then those who will witness His return in the sky.

As we've seen, that moment will mark the beginning of the end for this phase of human history. Once the Rapture occurs, our world will experience a seven-year countdown called the Tribulation that will end with *The End*—the Battle of Armageddon. Any person who has not yet accepted God's free gift of salvation at that point will run out of time. The option will be closed. If we procrastinate until the opportunity is gone, it will be All. Our. Fault.

The Bible ends with a final warning—a last invitation to come to Christ. You'll find it on the last page of the last book of the Bible: "Let him who thirsts come. Whoever desires, let him take the water of life freely" (Revelation 22:17). Those may be the most important words that you'll ever read.

Your Invitation Is Ready

Who has the option to accept the riches of salvation through Christ? Anyone. Everyone! And yes, that certainly includes you! Yes, heaven is restricted to those people who accept the Gospel of Jesus Christ. But there are no restrictions when it comes to responding to that Gospel. "For 'whoever calls on the name of the LORD shall be saved'" (Romans 10:13).

In my decades as a servant of Jesus, I've had the privilege of sharing the Gospel with thousands of people—many of them face to face. Often that message is received with joy—with eyes that brighten and lips that twitch upward into a smile of joy.

Sometimes, though, the person hearing the Gospel lowers their head. Their eyes go to the floor, and they sigh with such weight and such sadness that it breaks my heart every time. Even when they don't say the words out loud, I know exactly what they're thinking: It's not for me. If you only knew what I've done. If you only knew what was done to me. If you only knew what I'm capable of. I don't qualify. No! None of us qualify, and that's the point. That's the beauty of the Gospel.

You don't have to be perfect to qualify for salvation. You don't have to be above average or ahead of the curve to pass through the gates of heaven—more good things than bad things on your ledger. You don't have to be good or pure or nice, nor do you have to be a certain age or a certain color or live in a certain place.

If you want to know God, if you want to experience His love and grace, and if you want to enjoy fellowship with Him for all eternity—all you have to be is thirsty. Remember the words of Jesus' last invitation: "Let the one who is thirsty come; and let the one who wishes take the free gift of the water of life" (Revelation 22:17 NIV).

Many Bible translations say, "Whoever desires, let him come." Richard Baxter once wrote about the wonder of that word. "I thank God," he said, "for the word 'whosoever.' If God had said that there was mercy for Richard Baxter, I am so vile a sinner that I would have thought he meant some other Richard Baxter; but when he says 'whosoever' I know that it includes me, the worst of all Richard Baxters."[2]

I know "whoever" includes me. "David Jeremiah desires, so let him come." I've tasted of that living water, which is why I feel such eager anticipation for everything that is yet to come. Whether my journey takes me through the doorway of death or through the thrill of the Rapture, I know I will be with Christ.

Do you know? Have you tasted? If your answer is no, it's not too late—but time is short.

Your Response Is Required

As we've seen, there are no restrictions around the offer of salvation. But the Gospel does require something of everyone in need of living water. Revelation 22:17 says, "Let him take the water of life freely."

The only thing a thirsty person has to do is reach out and take the water. It's available to all, but we must make the choice to drink. You must make that choice.

Is it really that easy? We feel there must be something significant we have to say. There must be something more we have to do. We think there must be some level of maturity or goodness we have to attain—some kind of schooling or education we have to undergo.

No! Just come and drink. That's not a form of good works; it's just God's goodness and His grace. Reaching out and receiving a gift doesn't mean I did anything to earn the gift. The gift is offered freely—that's what makes it a gift. The response of the thirsty person is simply to take that which is offered freely by grace. The apostle Paul wrote, "For by grace you have been saved through faith, and that not of yourselves, it is the gift of God" (Ephesians 2:8).

If there was anything you could do to help yourself get saved even a little bit, do you think God in heaven would have sent Jesus Christ to this earth to die on the Cross for your sin? If there was any human way you could merit salvation or recommend yourself to God, do you think He would have paid the high price He did by giving His own Son as a sacrifice?

God sent Jesus Christ into this world because there's not a single thing any of us can do to save ourselves—nothing except to take the living water freely offered to us. We use various terms to refer to this process—belief, trust, commitment—but it means the same as "taking" the living water and drinking deeply.

The prophet Isaiah said, "Is anyone thirsty? Come and drink—even if you have no money! Come, take your choice of wine or milk—it's all free! Why spend your money on food that does not give you strength? Why pay for food that does you no good? Listen to me, and you will eat what is good. You will enjoy the finest food" (Isaiah 55:1–2 NLT).

The apostle John borrowed from Isaiah's words to craft the final invitation of the Bible. "Whoever desires, let him take the water of life freely" (Revelation 22:17).

Don't neglect to exercise your option, for this is truly the Bible's last word on the subject. The Rapture is real. Right now it is one day nearer than yesterday—one breath closer than your last exhalation. There is a moment in the future when all options will be removed and all fates sealed. We have to pray sincerely in a definite act of faith, "Dear Lord, I confess my sins, I'm so thirsty on the inside of my life, and I now receive Jesus Christ—the Living Water. Come into my life and help me live for You from this day forth!"

Presbyterian evangelist Benjamin Mills told of a friend of his, a pastor, who was preaching one night in his church. He invited people to come and kneel at the front of the room if they wanted to receive Christ as Savior. Several did so, and the pastor started to kneel and pray with them. But suddenly he was impressed to stand up and say he thought there was at least one more person who needed to come. Instantly, a young lady rose from the back seat and hurried forward, kneeling with the others and giving herself to Christ.

Two weeks later, this woman suffered a sudden fatal illness. On her deathbed, she said to the pastor, "I shall be glad through all eternity that you gave that last invitation that led me to Christ."[3]

Oh, you'll be thankful through all eternity that Jesus has given you one last invitation. I'm going to ask you as if I were sitting there beside you: Have you taken the living water which God offers in the person of Christ?

The Bible says, "Whoever calls on the name of the LORD shall be saved" (Romans 10:13). Let "whoever" be you!

APPLICATION

Personal Questions

1. Have you ever missed an opportunity because you failed to respond? Why did you not respond to the opportunity?

2. Where in the Bible is the last invitation to eternal life located? What does it say?

3. Have you ever thought that the Gospel is not for you? Why or why not?

4. Personalize Revelation 22:17 by rewriting it in the space below. Write your name where the word "whoever" appears.

5. According to Revelation 22:17, what does the Gospel require?

6. What do you think it means to take and drink deeply of "the water of life"?

7. Read Isaiah 55:1–2.

   a. How much money does God charge us to quench our spiritual thirst?

b. What does God promise to give us when we come to Him?

8. Have you personally responded to the last invitation in the Bible?

Group Questions

1. Share with the group about a time when you failed to respond to an important invitation and what happened because of that.

2. If applicable, share with the group about a time when you thought the Gospel was not for you.

3. Discuss some ways you can help people in your life understand that Revelation 22:17 applies to them. Together, think of other Scripture passages that communicate this truth.

4. Read Revelation 22:17 as a group.

   a. According to this verse, what does the Gospel require?

   b. Discuss what it means to take and drink deeply of "the water of life."

5. Read Romans 10:9–13 together.

   a. What do these verses teach us about salvation?

   b. Discuss the importance of "whoever" in verse 13.

6. How have you personally responded to the last invitation in the Bible? How can you encourage others to respond?

DID YOU KNOW?

Salt is a preservative, but it also creates thirst. Ranchers often give their cattle blocks of salt to lick so they will drink more water. That is a picture of our purpose as salt in the world, to make the spiritual thirst of people around us so strong that they reach out for the living water which Christ offers. The reason to emphasize Christlikeness is, first of all, out of obedience to God. But when we do that, we so distinguish ourselves from the world that their thirst for living water becomes stronger when they see our life. The reason people come to Christ is that they are thirsty and discover that He *is*—not just He *has*—Living Water.

Notes
   1. Belinda Luscombe, *Marriageology: The Art and Science of Staying Together* (New York, NY: Random House, 2019), 90.
   2. Richard Baxter, quoted in Bryan Chapell, *The Wonder of It All: Rediscovering the Treasure of Your Faith* (Wheaton, IL: Crossway Books, 1999), 189.
   3. Benjamin Fay Mills, "The After-Meeting: Drawing the Net," *Independent 47*, no. 2425 (May 23, 1895), 2.

WHY STUDY PROPHECY?

ISAIAH 46:9–11

*In this lesson we learn how prophecy can give us
practical help in living the Christian life.*

Some people are apt to ignore the prophetic parts of Scripture in favor
of more "practical" passages about living the Christian life. Perhaps
they fall into the errors of thinking either that the events foretold have
mostly already come to pass or that the ones that are yet to occur will happen with or without our assistance, so why bother worrying about them?
But prophecy is about so much more than just predicting future events.
In this lesson, you'll discover the marvelous ways that prophecy can bolster
our faith, help us trust God and His Word, and yes, even give us practical
help in living the Christian life.

OUTLINE

I. Prophecy Pervades Scripture

II. Prophecy Proves God's Sovereignty

OVERVIEW

Sadly, many people in our world, including Christians, think of biblical prophecy as interesting in some ways but not particularly useful or applicable to "real life." It has been said that Christians treat prophecy like the priest and the Levite treated the wounded man in the parable of the good Samaritan: They pass by on the other side. Some avoid prophecy because it seems difficult to understand. Others feel too overwhelmed by the present to think about the future.

While many Christians are content to leave prophecy's pages shrouded in mystery and misunderstanding, the fact remains it is our only reliable source of information about tomorrow. God alone knows the end from the beginning, and He foretells the future with absolute accuracy. Incredibly, He has chosen to share many of those foretellings with us, if we will only heed what they say.

Consider this illustration from the book *Armageddon, Oil, and Terror:*

Have you ever driven down a strange dark road in a blinding rainstorm? Every minute you wish you could see beyond the edge of the headlights to see what's ahead. If only you could know what was coming next—could intuitively know what's out there or predict what you'll find at the next bend in the road. We long to see ahead, to know, perhaps to avert disaster.

Can someone see what's ahead by intuition or a special gift? Can a prophet know the future because the path of our lives is part of a larger drama scripted ahead of time? This is what the prophets of the Bible claim. Can we know where we are in that pattern of events foretold by prophets, written in Scripture or seen in apocalyptic visions of the future? In the uncertain storm of the days in which we live, all of us yearn to see beyond the headlights.[1]

Only biblical prophecy allows you to do that!

Given these realities, here are just a few other reasons why it's worth our time as believers in Jesus to study biblical prophecy—including the Rapture.

Prophecy Pervades Scripture

Perhaps the main reason why we should study biblical prophecy is that there wouldn't be much of the Bible left if we tried to ignore its predictive passages. Prophecy is pervasive throughout all of Scripture.

In their book *Christ's Prophetic Plans*, John MacArthur and Richard Mayhue have done excellent work in identifying just how much of the Bible is prophetic. Here are a few examples of what they found:

- Sixty-two of the Bible's 66 books contain predictive information, with Ruth, Song of Solomon, Philemon, and 3 John as the only exceptions. That's 94 percent.
- Breaking things down even further, there are a total of 31,124 verses in Scripture. Incredibly, 27 percent of those verses (8,352) refer to prophetic issues. And 22 percent of all prophetic verses refer to Christ's Second Coming.
- Looking specifically at the End Times, there are approximately 333 specific biblical prophecies dealing with Christ's two advents. One-third describe His first coming, and two-thirds are connected to His Second Coming.[2]

If you value the Bible, then you need to value biblical prophecy.

Prophecy Proves God's Sovereignty

Have you ever wished you could prove that God is who He says He is? That His Word is relevant and meaningful for our life today?

You can! The prophetic passages of Scripture offer direct evidence that God knows everything and is in charge of everything. He is never surprised by anything, and whatever He says He will do, He does. He is sovereign, and He further proves that sovereignty every time His prophecies are fulfilled.

God Himself encouraged us to bank on the reliability of biblical prophecy in the book of Isaiah. "Remember the things I have done in the past. For I alone am God! I am God, and there is none like me. Only I can tell you the future before it even happens. Everything I plan will come to pass, for I do whatever I wish. . . . I have said what I would do, and I will do it" (Isaiah 46:9–11 NLT).

When we know the One who declares the beginning from the end, we can live every day with confidence.

Prophecy Promotes the Bible's Integrity

The confirmed accuracy of biblical prophecy boosts our confidence in God's sovereignty, and also in His Word. The more we study and understand the inerrancy of the Bible's prophetic passages, the more we trust every word of His Word.

Jesus used prophecy to validate His Messiahship, for example. This is what He said to His disciples:

- "I tell you this beforehand, so that when it happens you will believe that I am the Messiah" (John 13:19 NLT).
- "I have told you these things before they happen so that when they do happen, you will believe" (John 14:29 NLT).

Not only did Jesus perfectly prophesy about the future; He Himself was the fulfillment of prophecy. In the fullness of time, Jesus satisfied every detail of the prophets' predictions concerning the Messiah. He was a descendant of Abraham and the tribe of Judah (see Genesis 12:3; 49:10). He came from David's family line (see Isaiah 9:7) and was born in Bethlehem (see Micah 5:2). His name was Immanuel; He was born of a virgin (see Isaiah

7:14). He based His ministry in Galilee, spoke in parables, and did wonders among the people (see Isaiah 9:1–2; 6:9–10; 61:1–2). He was betrayed, pierced for our sins, and crucified with criminals (see Zechariah 11:12–13; Isaiah 53:5, 12). After His burial in a wealthy man's tomb, He rose again (see Isaiah 53:9–11).

Not a single one of the 13 billion or so people who have lived on earth could even come close to fulfilling the 109 prophecies fulfilled by Christ. He stands alone in human history, and He stands on the foundation of God's prophetic Word. The study of Messianic prophecy is a remarkable journey into ironclad evidence for the integrity of Scripture.[3]

Prophecy Protects Us From False Teaching

One of the main reasons Jesus prophesied about the End Times was to protect us from false teaching. In Matthew 24:4–5, He warned, "Take heed that no one deceives you. For many will come in My name, saying, 'I am the Christ,' and will deceive many." This warning is so essential that Scripture repeats it in Mark 13 and Luke 21.

We live in a day when deception is common. Jesus said in John 16:1, "These things I have spoken to you, that you should not be made to stumble." Knowing what the Bible says about the future protects us from being deceived.

As much as God wants to place us under prophecy's umbrella of protection, the devil wants to keep us out. Satan knows that reading 2 Thessalonians 2 will reveal his scheme to spread apostasy in the Last Days. And if we read Revelation 20, it will tell us that God has already assigned him to the lake of fire. Seeing Satan as a defeated foe in the future helps us to be victorious over him today. Prophecy protects us from Satan's attacks.

Prophecy Prepares Us for the Last Days

One of the great prophetic themes in the Bible is that God has a plan for history. That plan has phases, and the next phase is imminent. It can arrive at any moment.

Jesus told several parables to illustrate the importance of being prepared for His coming. One story was about a master of the house who had been robbed. If the master had known when the thief would come, he would have watched to prevent the robbery. The lesson is simple—be prepared. Always be ready for the Rapture, which will be as unpredictable as a thief in the night (see 1 Thessalonians 5:4).

Studying prophecy helps us prepare for the days ahead. Hardly a day goes by that we don't read about wars, rumors of wars, natural disasters, or lawlessness in the news. These grim realities can be disheartening. However, Jesus told His disciples to anticipate these events, that they would be signs that His return was on the horizon.

Tragedies never take God by surprise. Jesus said, "These things I have told you, that when the time comes, you may remember that I told you of them" (John 16:4). Studying Bible prophecy gives us courage in chaotic times. Although life on earth will continue to get worse, the day of the Rapture draws near.

Prophecy Provides Guidance for Every Day

All prophecy is by definition focused on the future. Yet it would be a mistake to conclude that biblical prophecy has no value for the present. Quite the opposite is true!

In the opening chapters of Revelation, one sentence appears seven times: "He who has an ear, let him hear what the Spirit says to the churches" (Revelation 2:7, 11, 17, 29; 3:6, 13, 22). In other words, "Listen up! I have something to say, and it's important." Prophecy contains practical instruction for every Christian, for every day.

In his book *World News and Bible Prophecy,* prophetic scholar Charles Dyer reminds us that "God gave prophecy to change our hearts, not to fill our heads with knowledge. God never predicted future events just to satisfy our curiosity about the future. He includes with His predictions practical applications to life. God's pronouncements about the future carry with them specific advice for the 'here and now.' "[4]

It would not be an exaggeration to say biblical prophecy drives evangelism and righteous living. Knowing what's coming encourages us to be ministry-oriented, reaching out to the lost.

Not only that, living with an awareness of Christ's imminent return increases our desire to share the Gospel. Prophecy elevates our perspective and energizes our walk with the Lord. God gave us prophecy to help us anticipate what is coming and to equip us for living in the world of the end.

Prophecy Promises Spiritual Blessing

Did you know that the book of Revelation is the only book in the Bible that promises a reward to its readers? This promise is found not just once, but twice.

- "Blessed is he who reads and those who hear the words of this prophecy, and keep those things which are written in it; for the time is near" (1:3).
- "Blessed is he who keeps the words of the prophecy of this book" (22:7).

The Bible forms a guidebook that teaches us the sequence of events leading up to the return of Jesus Christ. Biblical prophecy can seem complex, but it doesn't have to be confusing if we understand what Scripture's predictions mean for our life here and now.

John O'Neill worked for years as a counter-terrorism specialist for the FBI. He investigated many terrorist attacks, including the 1993 attack on the World Trade Center and various bombings throughout the Middle East. In the late 1990s, O'Neill developed serious concerns about the growing threat of Al Qaeda as an organization and of Osama bin Laden as its leader. O'Neill even prevented an Al Qaeda attack against the Los Angeles International Airport in 2000.

O'Neill shared his worries with U.S. officials. He even told the Associated Press in 1997, "A lot of these groups now have the capability and the support infrastructure in the United States to attack us here if they choose to do so." Sadly, his warnings were heard but not heeded. After retiring in August 2001, O'Neill accepted another position as chief of security at the World Trade Center. He was killed while attempting to help people evacuate the South Tower on September 11.[5]

The lesson from that story is that warnings are only helpful when they are acted upon. Knowledge of what's to come will only benefit us when we study it and allow it to influence our choices for today.

May that be the case for you and me. Let us never neglect the incredible gift we have received through the prophetic passages of God's Word.

APPLICATION

Personal Questions

1. How important is the study of biblical prophecy to you?

2. List three examples that show how pervasive prophecy is in the Bible.

3. How does Isaiah 46:9–11 describe God's sovereignty?

4. Read John 13:19 and 14:29. How did Jesus use prophecy in these verses?

5. List three prophecies that Jesus Himself fulfilled.

6. Where do you see deception in our world today? How does studying prophecy protect you from the lies of our culture?

7. How does studying prophecy give you more confidence as you prepare for the Last Days?

8. Read the following verses and write down the practical application connected to the return of the Lord. Reflect on the specific ways you can live out each of the verses.

    a. Hebrews 10:24–25

    b. James 5:7–8

    c. 1 John 2:28–29

    d. Jude 21–23

Group Questions

1. Discuss how important the study of biblical prophecy is for the Christian.

2. List some of the statistics about prophecy found in "Prophecy Pervades Scripture." Discuss what these facts tell us about the importance of prophecy.

3. Read John 13:19 and 14:29 together. What did Jesus tell His disciples in these verses?

4. Discuss some of the prophecies that Jesus Himself fulfilled.

5. In what ways does studying prophecy protect believers from the lies of our culture?

6. Share with the group how studying prophecy gives you more confidence as you prepare for the Last Days.

7. Read the following verses as a group and discuss the specific ways Christians can live out each of the verses.

   a. Hebrews 10:24–25

   b. James 5:7–8

   c. 1 John 2:28–29

   d. Jude 21–23

DID YOU KNOW?

In the book *Prophetic Messages for Modern Times*, Dr. Vance Havner described the importance of studying Bible prophecy this way: "Throughout the Word of God one thing stands out crystal clear in this matter of prophecy: wherever the Holy Spirit sets forth some great prophetic truth, He joins it every time with a practical exhortation as to what we are to do about it. The subject of prophecy has, of course, held an attraction for a great many superficial souls with a flair for the spectacular. . . . But then any good light will attract a certain number of bugs, so we need not be discouraged by the false to forget the truth. Certain it is that no Bible subject holds more practical implications than the matter of prophecy."[6]

Notes

1. John Walvoord and Mark Hitchcock, *Armageddon, Oil, and Terror* (Carol Stream, IL: Tyndale House Publishers, 2007), 1–2.

2. Richard Mayhue, "Introduction: Why Study Prophecy?," in *Christ's Prophetic Plans: A Futuristic Premillennial Primer*, ed. John Macarthur and Richard Mayhue (Chicago, IL: Moody Publishers, 2012), 14.

3. Tim LaHaye, *A Quick Look at the Rapture and the Second Coming* (Eugene, OR: Harvest House Publishers, 2013), 11.

4. Charles Dyer, *World News and Bible Prophecy* (Carol Stream, IL: Tyndale House Publishers, 1995), 270.

5. "John O'Neill's FBI Jacket and Passport Embody His Enduring Fight Against Terrorism," *9/11 Memorial and Museum*, https://www.911memorial.org/connect/blog/john-oneills-fbi-jacket-and-passport-embody-his-enduring-fight-against-terrorism.

6. Vance Havner, *Prophetic Messages for Modern Times*, ed. Robert J. Well (Charlottesville, VA: The University of Virginia, 1944), 1.

LEADER'S GUIDE

Thank you for your commitment to lead a group through *The Great Disappearance*. Being a leader has its own rewards. You may discover that your walk with the Lord deepens through this experience. Throughout the study guide, your group will explore new topics and review study questions that encourage thought-provoking group discussion.

The lessons in this study guide are suitable for Sunday school classes, small-group studies, elective Bible studies, or home Bible study groups. Each lesson is structured to provoke thought and help you grow in your knowledge and understanding of God. There are multiple components in this section that can help you structure your lessons and discussion time, so make sure you read and consider each one.

Before You Begin

Before you begin each meeting, make sure you and your group are well-versed with the content of the lesson. Group members should have their own study guide so they can follow along and write in the study guide if need be. You may wish to assign the study guide lesson as homework prior to the meeting of the group and then use the meeting time to discuss the lesson.

To ensure that everyone has a chance to participate in the discussion, the ideal size for a group is around eight to ten people. If there are more than ten people, try to break up the bigger group into smaller subgroups. Make sure the members are committed to participating each week, as this will help create stability and help you better prepare the structure of the meeting.

At the beginning of the study each week, start the session with a question to challenge group members to think about the issues you will be discussing. The members can answer briefly, but the goal is to have an idea in their mind as you go over the lesson. This allows the group members to become engaged and ready to interact with the group.

After reviewing the lesson, try to initiate a free-flowing discussion. Invite group members to bring questions and insights they may have discovered to the next meeting, especially if they were unsure of the meaning of some parts of the lesson. Be prepared to discuss how biblical truth applies to the world we live in today.

Weekly Preparation

As the group leader, here are a few things that you can do to prepare for each meeting:

- *Make sure you are thoroughly familiar with the material in the lesson.* Make sure you understand the content of the lesson so you know how to structure group time and are prepared to lead group discussion.

- *Decide, ahead of time, which questions you want to discuss.* Depending on how much time you have each week, you may not be able to reflect on every question. Select specific questions that you feel will evoke the best discussion.

- *Take prayer requests.* At the end of your discussion, take prayer requests from your group members and pray for each other.

Structuring the Discussion Time

As the group leader, it is up to you to keep track of the time and keep things moving along according to your schedule. If your group is having a good discussion, don't feel the need to stop and move on to the next question. Remember, the purpose is to pull together ideas and share unique insights on the lesson. Make time each week to discuss how to apply these truths to living for Christ today.

The purpose of discussion is for everyone to participate, but don't be concerned if certain group members are more quiet—they may be internally reflecting on the questions and need time to process their ideas before they can share them.

If you need help in organizing your time when planning your group Bible study, the following schedule, for sixty minutes and ninety minutes, can give you a structure for the lesson:

Section	60 Minutes	90 Minutes
WELCOME: Members arrive and get settled	5 minutes	10 minutes
GETTING STARTED QUESTION: Prepares the group for interacting with one another	10 minutes	10 minutes
MESSAGE: Review the lesson	15 minutes	25 minutes
DISCUSSION: Discuss group study questions	25 minutes	35 minutes
PRAYER AND APPLICATION : Final application for the week and prayer before dismissal	5 minutes	10 minutes

Group Dynamics

Leading a group study can be a rewarding experience for you and your group members—but that doesn't mean there won't be challenges. Certain members may feel uncomfortable discussing topics that they consider very personal and might be afraid of being called on. Some members might have disagreements on specific issues. To help prevent these scenarios, consider the following ground rules:

- If someone has a question that may seem off topic, suggest that it is discussed at another time, or ask the group if they are okay with addressing that topic.

- If someone asks a question you don't know the answer to, confess that you don't know and move on. If you feel comfortable, invite other group members to give their opinions or share their comments based on personal experience.

- If you feel like a couple of people are talking much more than others, direct questions to people who may not have shared yet. You could even ask the more dominating members to help draw out the quiet ones.

- When there is a disagreement, encourage the group members to process the matter in love. Invite members from opposing sides to evaluate their opinions and consider the ideas of the other members. Lead the group through Scripture that addresses the topic, and look for common ground.

When issues arise, encourage your group to think of Scripture: "Love one another" (John 13:34), "If it is possible, as far as it depends on you, live at peace with everyone" (Romans 12:18 NIV), and "Be quick to listen, slow to speak and slow to become angry" (James 1:19 NIV).

ABOUT
DR. DAVID JEREMIAH
AND TURNING POINT

Dr. David Jeremiah is the founder of Turning Point, a ministry committed to providing Christians with sound Bible teaching relevant to today's changing times through radio and television broadcasts, audio series, books, and live events. Dr. Jeremiah's common-sense teaching on topics such as family, prayer, worship, angels, and biblical prophecy forms the foundation of Turning Point.

David and his wife, Donna, reside in El Cajon, California, where he serves as the senior pastor of Shadow Mountain Community Church. David and Donna have four children and twelve grandchildren.

In 1982, Dr. Jeremiah brought the same solid teaching to San Diego television that he shares weekly with his congregation. Shortly thereafter, Turning Point expanded its ministry to radio. Dr. Jeremiah's inspiring messages can now be heard worldwide on radio, television, and the Internet.

Because Dr. Jeremiah desires to know his listening audience, he travels nationwide holding ministry events that touch the hearts and lives of many people. According to Dr. Jeremiah, "At some point in time, everyone reaches a turning point; and for every person, that moment is unique, an experience to hold onto forever. There's so much changing in today's world that sometimes it's difficult to choose the right path. Turning Point offers people an understanding of God's Word as well as the opportunity to make a difference in their lives."

Dr. David Jeremiah has authored numerous books, including *Escape the Coming Night* (Revelation), *The Handwriting on the Wall* (Daniel), *Prayer—The Great Adventure, Agents of the Apocalypse, Agents of Babylon, A Life Beyond Amazing, Overcomer, Everything You Need, Forward, Shelter in God, The Jesus You May Not Know, The God You May Not Know, Where Do We Go From Here?,* and *The World of the End.*

stay connected to the teaching of

DR. DAVID JEREMIAH

·········

Publishing | Radio | Television | Online

FURTHER YOUR STUDY OF THIS BOOK

• • • • • • • •

The Great Disappearance Resource Materials

To enhance your study on this important topic, we recommend the correlating audio message album, study guide, and DVD messages from *The Great Disappearance* series.

Audio Message Album

The material found in this book originated from messages presented by Dr. Jeremiah. These messages are conveniently packaged in an accessible audio album.

DVD Message Presentations

Watch Dr. Jeremiah deliver *The Great Disappearance* original messages in this special DVD collection.

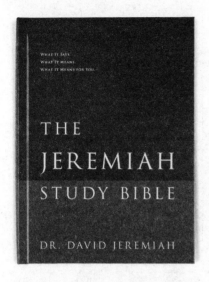

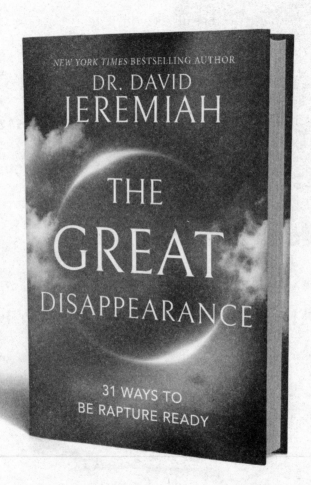

New Bible Study Series
from Dr. David Jeremiah

The Jeremiah Bible Study Series captures Dr. David Jeremiah's forty-plus years of commitment to teaching the whole Word of God. Each volume contains twelve lessons for individuals and groups to explore what the Bible says, what it meant to the people at the time it was written, and what it means to us today. Out of his lifelong ministry of *delivering the unchanging Word of God to an ever-changing world*, Dr. Jeremiah has written this Bible-strong study series focused not on causes, current events, or politics, but on the solid truth of Scripture.

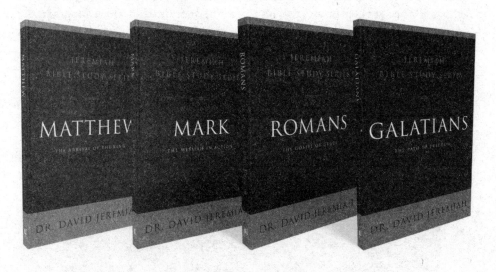

Available now at your favorite bookstore.

 Harper*Christian* Resources

This Is Our Time to Be the Answer

Some days it seems like bad news all around. And with bad news comes questions: "Why is this happening?" "When will it stop?" "Is this the end?"

In these hope-filled pages, bestselling author, pastor, and respected Bible teacher Dr. David Jeremiah will help you focus your mind on the hand of God instead of the problems at hand. Jesus Himself revealed what to expect from this season of history when He delivered His Olivet Discourse—a sermon that scholars have called "the most important single passage of prophecy in all the Bible."

This book and study guide focus on Jesus' prophecy in Matthew 24. Jesus makes it clear that all the signs He points to won't occur at once; instead, they will gradually appear and become stronger and more frequent. You will learn exactly what Jesus promised to us—and what He expects of us—as we approach the World of the End.

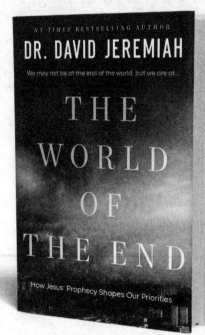

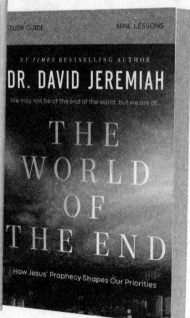

Hardcover
9780785251996

Bible Study Guide
9780310155928

Available now at your favorite bookstore.

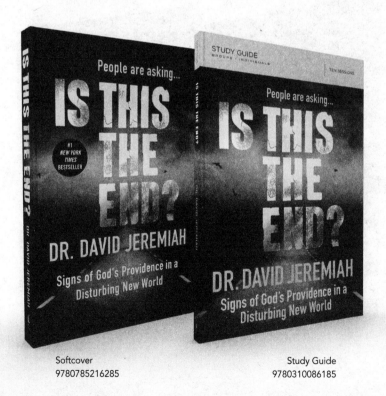

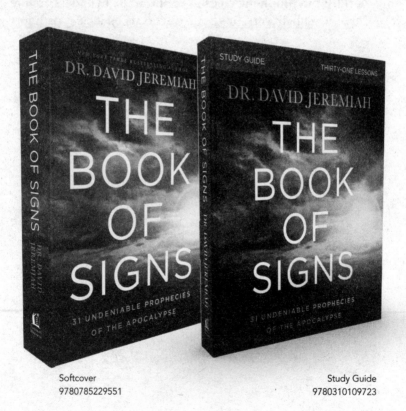